Age of

ARE WE THERE YET?

STEVE MAGILL

**AGE OF THE ANTICHRIST
ARE WE THERE YET?**
Published by Age*of*Antichrist.*com*
Copyright © November 2017
by Steve Magill
All rights reserved.

No part of this publication may be reproduced, stored in a retrieval system, or transmitted in any way by any means—electronic, mechanical, photocopy, recording, or otherwise—without the prior permission of the copyright holder, except as provided by USA copyright law.

Scripture quotations are from the King James Version unless otherwise noted. Author replaced some old English words with modern English, such as thee, thou, didst, etc.

Printed in the United States
by CreateSpace

ISBN-13: 978-1979354103
ISBN-10: 1979354103

"But take ye heed: behold,
I have foretold you
all things."
(Mark 13:23)

Dedicated to my daughter, Kellie,
and my grandmothers, Elva & Thelma,
who now experiences the hope
I press forward to gain

Contents

	Introduction	7
1	Are We There Yet?	11
2	Timeline 1	31
	Toward the Last Days	
3	Timeline 2	41
	Toward the Final Years	
4	Timelines 3 & 4	77
	The Countdown Begins	
5	Timeline 5	101
	Age of the Antichrist	
6	The Prophetic Timeline	113
7	Our Response	117
	Resources	168

Appendix A: Against All Odds	123
Appendix B: God of This World	135
Appendix C: Daniel 11 Commentary	147
Appendix D: The Key to Faith	155
Appendix E; Kings in Training	157

Timeline 1: Daniel 2	40
Timeline 2: Daniel 7	75
Timeline 3: Daniel 9	82
Timeline 4: Matthew 24	99
Timeline 5: Age of the Antichrist	112
The Prophetic Timeline	115

Chart: Devil's Body on Earth – Daniel 2	38
Chart: Devil's Body on Earth – Daniel 7	49
Chart: Earth's Final 10 ½ Years	63
Chart: Comparison of Last Day Events	95
Map: Club of Rome World Realignment	55
Map: United Nations World Realignment	56
Map: Israel & the Middle East	127

INTRODUCTION

Introduction

"LOOK AT ALL YOU HAVE TO GIVE UP."

THE VOICE WAS ANGRY...DESPERATE...COMING FROM WITHIN ME. I WAS FEARFUL, NOT QUITE UNDERSTANDING what was happening, yet knowing that I was in a life and death struggle with this voice within my head. It was more than just a voice; there was something very physical, very personal about this battle taking place within me.

What would I have to give up? It didn't matter. The fact that I was in this struggle made me realize that my decision to commit my life to Jesus on that early morning of December 1, 1976, proved that Jesus was real and what the Bible said about Him was true.

I didn't know what to do. I felt very much alone and afraid as I climbed into my bed, covered my head, and did the only thing I had been taught throughout childhood to do—call upon Jesus. "Jesus, Jesus, Jesus," I thought, then vocalized. The struggle of wills became more intense. My desperation became more desperate. I kept calling, "Jesus, Jesus, Jesus." After what felt to be a lengthy battle, I felt something on my feet. Peering over my covers, as I had done as a child, uncertain of what I might see, I cried out, "Jesus, Jesus, Jesus"...then again, over and over, "Jesus, Jesus, Jesus."

Fear held me. I lay motionless, glaring for but a second or two at the source of my battle sitting on my feet. As quickly as I saw it, it disappeared. It was the demon that was in me filled with anger and bitterness. I cried out again, "Jesus, Jesus, Jesus." It was then that peace and an overwhelming comfort penetrated every cell of my body. I smiled. I laughed. I experienced love. Jesus came. Jesus filled me with His Spirit and my life changed. Who I was prior to this early morning battle had disappeared. I was now on a journey from which, to this day, I have not turned back.

CHANGES

With this change of spirit also came many changes in my understanding of life and truth. One of these had to do with how the world was not moving toward bigger and better things, but to its end. Realizing that the end would dissolve humanity into an eternity of either God's kingdom or the lake of fire spurred me to encourage others to repent and turn toward Christ. A Scripture I've embraced since the early days of receiving Christ's love was Mark 1:15. This Scripture let me know that the world is moving toward its end, God's kingdom will replace our present world, and we need to repent and believe the message Jesus taught to prepare for eternity. My number one focus was now to encourage others

Introduction

to repent and prepare for Christ's return...that would change in 2005.

In 2005, twenty-nine years after committing my life to Christ, I experienced a very personal, knife-cutting side of the last days as I understood that the church would enter great apostasy and deception, where most claiming the name of Christ would have an image of being a Christian without the power of the Holy Spirit to actually be Christian. I've taught and preached this many times, but the reality of it all took on a new depth, a new intensity. This concept cut me deep as I realized that a person does not live in apostasy and deception knowing they have been deceived.

I began to question who I was as a Christian, whether I was a true Christian, who and what I was as a pastor, and was I really prepared to stand eyeball to eyeball with the God who created me? Certain Scriptures such as 2 Thessalonians 2:3, 2 Timothy 3:5, and Revelation chapters 2 and 3 would burn within me, unsettling the Christianity I had grown up with. Each of these Scriptures had to do with Christians thinking they were Christian when they were not Christian at all. Eventually I made changes which included stepping down from my position as a "professional pastor"[1] in 2008 to become a "normal," everyday Christian. This repentance was equivalent to my initial repentance over forty years ago. Forty years ago, I gave up sin; in 2008 I gave up everything I thought I knew about Christianity and the church.

After this change, I began to see an urgent side of the last days (2008 to the present). I realized, like never before,

---

[1] "Professional" is used in the sense that I worked in a denomination full-time, receiving from them a pay check, benefits, perks, retirement, etc.

ARE WE THERE YET?

that if I live a natural and long life, my eyes will see the Antichrist and experience the earth's last seven years. With this understanding, my focus shifted to helping others understand where we are on the prophetic timeline. Scriptures, such as Daniel 11:33 and Revelation 10:10-11, now spurs me on with their encouragement to teach prophecy to many.

Also spurring me on were the many conversations I've had about the last days and comments such as the one that Ron made:[2] "That's why Jesus came, right? To tell us about these things so we will know without a doubt?"

Ron was typical of so many I've discussed the last days with. He was not lacking knowledge of the events of these days: apostasy, the Antichrist, the great tribulation, the return of Christ. His pressing issue was: "Since Jesus came to tell us about the last days, gave us events to look for, and told us to be ready...then we should be able to know where we are, and whether we are there yet, right?"

Though Ron knew the events of the last days, he didn't know how to organize them into a roadmap to give assurance of where he was on the prophetic timeline. How was he to know, especially with all the contradicting teachings and books on the last days?

My goal in this book is to lay the foundation for understanding last day events through the lens of the prophetic/historical timelines outlined in the books of Daniel, Matthew, and Revelation.

---

[2] Ron is not his real name. The quotes are typical of numerous conversations I've had with others.

CHAPTER 1

Are We There Yet?
Understanding Prophecy

A SEARCH OF THE INTERNET WILL BRING UP INNUMERABLE ARTICLES ABOUT THE LAST DAYS. IT APPEARS EVERYONE HAS THEIR OWN VERSION OF HOW things will take place. What all these theories and postulating indicate is that there is not one foundation from which the theories originate. If there were, there would not be so many contradicting views concerning the last days. Somewhere along the way, we have moved past the "one mind and one doctrine" of the early church.[3]

This is to be expected in our age of apostasy and deception, since the Devil is the author of confusion and he is fulfilling his job description with excellence. One of his great achievements has been the dividing of the church into factions, called denominations, with most claiming to be the true guardians of Christianity. This lack of unity is no doubt

---

3 Acts 4:32; Philippians 1:27

one of the reasons many believe their opinion concerning the things of God are valid, just because it is *their* opinion. The difficulty is that all opinions and theories are not valid; to think otherwise is to throw aside absolute truth. This division of thought is contrary to Jesus' statement, "And ye shall know the truth, and the truth shall make you free."[4] If we can know the truth, why do we have so many "truths" that create divisions among those who claim the name of Christ? It appears we have departed from the One who leads into all truth, the Holy Spirit.[5] Our departure from the Holy Spirit will be looked at later in this chapter.

This division of truth has also moved us from understanding the truth of the last days. Since the events of the last days have to do with nations and political events, we must ask if there is a timeline of nations revealed in Scripture to move us through the last days. The unequivocal answer is yes. In the books of Daniel, Matthew, and Revelation we have measurable and dated timelines which move us through the last days to the return of Christ, so we can confidently answer the question, "Are we there yet?"

MUST BE OBSERVABLE

There are two other reasons why prophetic events are not understood. The first is because the events of prophecy must be observable before they can be known. The second is the lack of or disregard of the Holy Spirit's guidance who gives this understanding.

---

4 John 8:32
5 John 16:13

Are We There Yet?

Concerning the first reason, after Daniel was given his vision, he was then told:

> "But you, O Daniel, shut up the words, and seal the book, even to the time of the end: many shall run to and fro, and knowledge shall be increased."[6]

This statement is clear that understanding will not be given until the end times are here. We will know we are at the end when these two events are observable, everyday events.

These two events will set the stage for the time of trouble that the two angels told Daniel would take place and last for three and a half years,[7] taking place when the Antichrist is on the scene. This is the time when God's anger toward Israel will be completed.[8] This is speaking of the future Antichrist who will scatter and cause great persecution upon God's people. In other words, the end will not take place until the Antichrist unleashes the great tribulation.

Daniel heard what must have been overwhelming to him. He wanted to know when these things would take place and asked the angels: "What shall be the end of these things?"[9] Daniel was told to go back to his day-to-day activities. This knowledge would not be given since the vision would be closed and sealed until the generation in which

---

6 Daniel 12:4
7 Daniel 12:1-7
8 Daniel 12:7b
9 Daniel 12:8

they would be fulfilled;[10] this generation would be the "this generation" of Matthew 24. Understanding of last day events would not be given until far into Daniel's future.

Though the unrighteous will not understand what is taking place or why, those who are wise and belong to God will understand.[11] God's people are able to understand the times they are living in and where they are on the prophetic timeline.

The two main events letting us know we are in the last of the last days is when knowledge and travel increases. Along with these, wickedness will increase, the Antichrist will appear, and the temple will be rebuilt. According to Daniel, we will know when we enter the last of the last days when the following events are observable:

1. Exponential increase in travel (Dan. 12:4)
2. Exponential increase in knowledge (Dan. 12:4)
3. The Antichrist appears and persecutes God's people (Dan. 12:7)
4. Wickedness and sin would be great (Dan. 12:10)
5. The temple would be rebuilt (Dan. 12:11)

Out of these five events only two have not been fulfilled in our present generation: the rebuilding of the temple and the appearance of the Antichrist. The other three stand as witnesses to the fulfillment of Daniel's vision. Here's a brief

---

10 Daniel 12:8-9
11 Daniel 12:10

Are We There Yet?

synopsis of the increase in these events since the twentieth century.

First, *"Many shall run to and fro."*[12] No one can deny that we are the most traveling generation in all of recorded history. It was country singer Willie Nelson who captured this spirit when he sings: "On the road again/ Goin' places that I've never been/Seein' things that I may never see again/And I can't wait to get on the road again."

Like swarms of bees, we flit from city to city, state to state, nation to nation. When you consider that from Daniel's time until the mid 1800s (over 2,500 years) travel consisted of horseback, wagons, and boats, and that people only traveled a few miles from their home at most, it is without question that this is the fulfillment of Daniel 12:4.

Second, *"Knowledge shall increase."*[13] Who can deny the great explosion of knowledge concerning everything under the sun, secular and religious, visible and invisible, that exploded in the twentieth century? Consider that before the twentieth century, knowledge of modern technology and the availability of knowledge just didn't exist. Consider also the explosion of universities, state colleges, community colleges, correspondence schools, seminars, conferences, and online classes.

No one can deny that our time in recorded history is the only time when knowledge has become so available that it is frequently called "the information age." It has been said that a week's worth of the New York Time's contains more

---

[12] Daniel 12:4
[13] Ibid.

information than someone would be exposed to in a lifetime in the 1800's. One author explains this explosion of knowledge in this way:

> "...until 1900 human knowledge doubled approximately every century. By the end of World War II knowledge was doubling every 25 years. Today things are not as simple as different types of knowledge have different rates of growth. For example, nanotechnology knowledge is doubling every two years and clinical knowledge every 18 months. But on average human knowledge is doubling every 13 months. According to IBM, the build out of the 'internet of things' will lead to the doubling of knowledge every 12 hours."[14]

This increase of knowledge in our times is without question the fulfillment of Daniel 12:4.

Third, *"The wicked shall do wickedly."*[15] This phrase is a contrast to the one before it, speaking of how many of God's people "shall be purified, and made white, and tried."[16] In contrast, the wicked will continue to do wickedly with more people being involved with more sin. This also is brought out in Jesus' teaching on the last days when he taught:

> "And because iniquity shall abound, the love of many shall wax cold."[17]

---

14 David Russell Schilling, "Knowledge Doubling Every 12 Months, Soon to be Every 12 Hours," April 19, 2013. www.industrytap.com/knowledge-doubling-every-12-months-soon-to-be-every-12-hours/3950
15 Daniel 12:10
16 Daniel 12:10
17 Matthew 24:12

Are We There Yet?

Today we are eyewitnesses to how iniquity abounds with more people doing wickedly with the killing of our babies in the name of abortion, the mind-altering drug, marijuana, legalized as a recreational pleasure, and the legalizing of various deviant acts by calling them a disease or a choice. Sadly, the world's culture is being turned upside down where what was once seen as wrong is now called right and the right is increasingly being called wrong.[18]

Great wickedness and sin have always raised its ugly head throughout history. We only need to bring in remembrance the legalization of child sex with adults, slavery, and all kinds of vices running rampant and tolerated in England as recent as the 1800's. And who could forget the atrocities of Stalin, Hitler, and Genghis Khan, as well as the ongoing exploits of the Islamic State in our present age?

What makes wickedness a sign of the last days is that it will not be localized to certain countries and people, but will permeate the entire world to return us to the days of Noah, before the flood, when sin and violence permeated the earth corrupting all people.[19] Also, sin will no longer be hidden behind closed doors or seen as being undesirable. Sin will be open, accepted, and viewed as part of the normal human experience.

This time of great wickedness we are presently moving toward is what the Apostle Paul calls "perilous times."[20] It will be a time when the Christian love of many will grow

---

18 Isaiah 5:20
19 Genesis 6:11,12
20 2 Timothy 3:1

weak because of widespread sin.[21] Though many think we are now living in these perilous times, things will grow much worse as we move closer to the age of the Antichrist.

Fourth, *"Many shall be purified and made white, and tried."*[22] No one likes to think that one day their name may appear in a future edition of *Foxes Christian Martyrs,* but the reality is that persecution and Christianity fit together like a hand in glove.[23]

As we move closer to the arrival of the Antichrist, persecution will continue to increase and become more intense and frequent until it brings us into the great tribulation.[24] Though it hasn't yet reached the level Daniel speaks of, many articles indicate that global persecution of Christians is intensifying and moving toward what is known as the "great tribulation." What makes this tribulation greater than any we've experienced at any other time in history is that it will permeate the entire earth, not just certain countries or particular people.

Statistics suggest that Christianity is now the most persecuted religion in the world, with estimates of over 100 million Christians presently persecuted because of their faith.[25] In some parts of the world, such as the Middle East,

---

21 Matthew 24:12
22 Daniel 12:10
23 2 Timothy 3:12; John 15:20
24 Matthew 24:21
25 "The Persecution of Christians Is Increasing, "Voice of the Persecuted September 11, 2013.
voiceofthepersecuted.wordpress.com/2013/11/09/the-persecution-of-christians-is-increasing/

Are We There Yet?

there is the concern whether or not the church will survive.[26] What this persecution looks like is described by one author in this way:

> "From all accounts, the incidents of persecution are now apparently relentless and worsening; churches being burnt, Christians under pressure to convert, mob violence against Christian homes, abduction and rape of Christian girls, anti-Christian propaganda in the media and from Government, discrimination in schools and the work place...the list goes on." [27]

This increase in persecution in Daniel 12:10 is being fulfilled. What is the purpose of persecution? As unsettling as this may be, Daniel 12:10 reveals that persecution and martyrdom are used of God to purify, to make righteous, to revive and preserve His remnant.[28] Like a glove protects the hand, so does persecution protect and preserve the faith of God's people. Throughout history, Christianity has always thrived during times of persecution. This is exemplified when the Israelites were in captivity in Egypt; the more they were persecuted, the more they grew.[29]

---

26 "Christian Persecution has Increased in 20 Countries," UCAN Indica October 21, 2013. www.ucanews.com/news/christian-persecution-has-increased-in-20-countries/69515

27 "One Third of Syrian Christians Have Gone, Says Cleric," Open Doors October 24, 2013

28 The Apostle James expresses this same sentiment when he wrote in James 1:2-4: "My brethren, count it all joy when ye fall into divers temptations; Knowing this, that the trying of your faith works patience. But let patience have her perfect work, that ye may be perfect and entire, wanting nothing." Trials, troubles, and tribulation leads to being purified and perfected.

29 Exodus 1:12

ARE WE THERE YET?

Fifth, *"The temple is to be rebuilt."* In order for the end time abomination of desolation to be set up in the temple, it must be rebuilt, since it is not now in existence.[30] Are there plans in place right now for the rebuilding of the temple? The plans and all that is necessary to rebuild the temple and restart temple worship and sacrifices are in place. It is now up to God to permit the Antichrist to establish peace with Israel and her enemies in order for the rebuilding to begin. For more information concerning the plans for rebuilding the temple, visit templeinstitute.org.

These five events, happening at the same time, is one more confirmation that we have entered that time revealed to Daniel as the end. It is with the arrival of these exponential events that make it possible to understand the end times. It was not possible to understand the books of Daniel or Revelation until these events appeared. This indicates that our theories concerning the last days prior to this time must be seen as either incomplete or perhaps completely wrong. Now that Daniel's prophecies are being fulfilled in our present age, understanding where we are on the prophetic timeline is possible. Confusion no longer has to be the norm.

---

[30] The temple that Ezra had built was also defiled by Antiochus Epiphanes before the Roman Empire came into existence. Also, Titus, the Roman Prince, defiled the temple before he destroyed it in 70 AD. Yet neither of these fulfilled all the criteria that this future end time abomination would fulfill.

Are We There Yet?

MUST HAVE THE HOLY SPIRIT

The second, and number one reason there is confusion about where we are on the prophetic timeline today, is that the majority claiming the name of Christ are not connected with the Holy Spirit.

It is the Holy Spirit that gives understanding of the things of God. When we are connected to the Holy Spirit, our understanding of the things of God is much greater than that which the well educated in book learning and the world's wisdom have. This is brought out in Matthew 11:25 when Jesus prayed:

> "I thank You, Father, Lord of heaven and earth, that You have hidden these things from the wise and prudent and have revealed them to babes."

This concept of babes should be a mind blower for each of us. It is a term referring to someone who is not yet mature, just beginning, starting to learn, and growing; in this case, it refers to their knowledge of the things concerning God. It was this concept Jesus used to contrast those embracing Christianity with those mature in the wisdom and knowledge of the things belonging to the world. Those belonging to Christ are in contact with a knowledge that is different from that belonging to the world. It is knowledge hand-delivered by the Holy Spirit from the mind of God.

The Holy Spirit is an actual part of God, and He knows all things. He is within God's people and the knowledge that is within Him is within us, because He is within us.[31] Though we have the knowledge of all things does not mean we have complete knowledge within our consciousness. It is required that we search out that knowledge within, as Proverbs 25:2 encourages:

> "It is the glory of God to conceal a thing: but the honor of kings is to search out a matter."

You and I are kings in training. It should be the greatest of delights to search out the truths given from the King of Kings.[32]

This knowledge from the Holy Spirit is the knowledge the Jewish people perceived in Jesus when, in amazement, they spoke, "How does this man know letters, having never learned?"[33] In Acts 4:13, the rulers, elders, and scribes observed in the disciples a knowledge that surpassed their education: "Now when they saw the boldness of Peter and John, and perceived that they were unlearned and ignorant men, they marveled; and they took knowledge of them, that they had been with Jesus." It is this knowledge, hand-delivered by God, which allows you and I to "understand that the worlds were framed by the word of God, so that things which are seen were not made of things which do appear."[34] It is this knowledge from God that caused the Apostle Peter to proclaim, "You are the Christ, the Son of the living God," and caused Jesus to respond, "Blessed are you, Simon

---

31 1 John 2:20
32 Psalm 1:1-3
33 John 7:15
34 Hebrews 11:3

Are We There Yet?

Barjona: for flesh and blood has not revealed it to you, but my Father which is in heaven."[35]

The knowledge given to God's people is that knowledge which does not come from book learning and formal education, but directly from the hand of God. It is this knowledge that can only be received by God's people as 1 Corinthians 2:11-14 makes clear:

> "For what man knows the things of a man, save the spirit of man which is in him? even so the things of God knows no man, but the Spirit of God. Now we have received, not the spirit of the world, but the spirit which is of God; that we might know the things that are freely given to us of God. Which things also we speak, not in the words which man's wisdom teaches, but which the Holy Ghost teaches; comparing spiritual things with spiritual. But the natural man receives not the things of the Spirit of God: for they are foolishness unto him: neither can he know them, because they are spiritually discerned."

This knowledge from the Holy Spirit is where the Apostle John received understanding of earth's last seven years in the book of Revelation. He was *in the Spirit*, meaning that the Spirit of God was strong with John and was permitting him to see the revelation through pictures and sounds as if he were actually witnessing the Antichrist and the day of the Lord.[36] It was not through much study and observation that John received discernment of the final years of earth's history, but through an outside force, the Holy Spirit.

---

35 Matthew 16:16-17
36 Revelation 1:10

ARE WE THERE YET?

The prophet Daniel also received his knowledge of the last days, not from much study and knowledge, but from visions, dreams, and angels. While seeking knowledge and understanding got him into the books, understanding and discernment of the reality of this knowledge was hand-delivered by God.[37]

Please don't misunderstand me. We are not to throw book knowledge aside. We are encouraged to study to show ourselves approved unto God, to meditate, and to think upon the things of God.[38] However, without the Holy Spirit to give discernment, we will never truly understand God's knowledge or where we are on the prophetic timeline. This lack of knowledge from the Holy Spirit is the number one reason there is so much confusion concerning the last days in our present age. Think about this in this light: if the Holy Spirit is giving the knowledge of all the contradicting opinions, then why is He so confused? I don't think it is the Holy Spirit who is confused. I do think that many claiming the name of Christ are not in tune with Him. It appears the apostasy of our present age is greater than most of us are willing to admit.

NO ONE REALLY KNOWS, RIGHT?

In my discussions concerning the prophetic/historical timeline, inevitably someone will say, "It could take place this year or may not take place for another hundred or thousand

---

37 Daniel 2:27-28; 7:1; 8:1; 9:21-22; 10:1
38 2 Timothy 2:15; Psalm 1:1-3; Philippians 4:8

years...nobody really knows." This uncertainty is not what Scripture teaches. We are meant to know.

When Jesus told us to "watch," He was telling us to observe what was happening in the world around us. When we see social, cultural, political, and religious happenings aligning themselves with prophetic events, then we can know where we are on the prophetic/historical timeline. Jesus was clear that the events He outlined in Matthew 24 would let us know where we are on the prophetic timeline when He told His disciples, "When ye shall see all these things, know that it is near, even at the doors."[39]

As the great deceiver and liar, the Devil adds great confusion to God's word,[40] especially during our time in history when understanding of prophetic events would be given. Therefore, we should give even more diligence to the words given to the Apostle John in Revelation 1:3 where we are encouraged:

> "Blessed is he that reads and they that hears the words of this prophecy and keeps those things that are written therein."

The encouragement here is to read, hear, and keep. It is difficult to keep what we do not understand; therefore we must be students of God's Word and truly connect with the Holy Spirit. This verse indicates we can understand (hear), we can know (be certain), and we are able to keep (guard, preserve, protect) ourselves from the Devil's wiles and deceptions. The encouragement here is to read, hear, and

---

[39] Matthew 24:33
[40] John 8:44; 2 Corinthians 11:3, 14; John 8:44; Revelation 12:9

ARE WE THERE YET?

keep the prophecy given in the book of Revelation. This final prophecy is the key to understanding with certainty last day events. God has always given this certainty to His people. Amos 3:7 gives this assurance:

> "Surely the Lord God will do nothing, but he reveals his secret unto his servants the prophets."

Revelation 19:10 gives this incredible thought: "The testimony of Jesus is the spirit of prophecy."

This means that every Christian has the ability to know where they are on the prophetic timeline because they have an actual part of God in them, communicating with them. It is this Holy Spirit that made a prophet a spokesman for God. It is this Holy Spirit that makes you and I proclaimers of God's truth. It is this Holy Spirit that allows you and I to know where we are on God's prophetic timeline.

Anytime God moves within the world, He lets His people know before it happens. Noah is a good example of this. God told Noah that the world he knew would end, when it would end (in 120 years), and what he was to do to prepare for this end.[41]

Later, God revealed to the prophets that the Messiah would come and taught that the Messiah would appear, when He would appear, and what signs to watch for to know He had arrived. And then there is the Messiah Himself who told His disciples that the present age would end, when it would

---

41 Genesis 6:11-22

Are We There Yet?

end, and what signs to watch for to know that our present age is in its final years.[42]

Does it really make sense that God would inform Noah, the prophets, the disciples, and not leave with us the same certainty? Let us remember that the majority did not hear God's voice or understand the signs that Noah understood. In Jesus' day, the majority did not discern the signs that the wise men followed to give gifts to the Christ child. Very few discern the prophetic time they are living in. Jesus' rebuke, in Luke 12:54-56, of the people of His day confirms there is no excuse for not knowing the prophetic times we are living in.

> "And he said also to the people, When ye see a cloud rise out of the west, straightway ye say, There comes a shower; and so it is. And when ye see the south wind blow, ye say, There will be heat; and it comes to pass. Ye hypocrites, ye can discern the face of the sky and of the earth; but how is it that ye do not discern this time?"

The Messiah had come. Prophesy was fulfilled before their eyes. Yet they did not know where they were on the prophetic timeline. The conclusion to the matter is that prophecy is not given as an intellectual or philosophical pursuit. Prophesy is given to give assurance of where we are on the prophetic timeline. Prophecy is given so we can confidently answer the question, "Are we there yet?"

IN CLOSING

The main hindrance to understanding anything that is of God is the lack of a connection to the Holy Spirit. Without the

---

[42] Matthew 24:4-37

ARE WE THERE YET?

Holy Spirit, the things belonging to God cannot be understood.

In this light, I think of my grandmother who only had a sixth-grade education. She could not explain the latest theological term, but she understood theology. She could not quote Scripture word for word, but she knew the Word of God. She could not articulate the right and wrong of a situation, but she knew right from wrong. In all of her earthly weakness, she was strong in spiritual discernment and knowledge. In our churches today, it appears we are strong in earthly wisdom and knowledge, but weak in the discernment and knowledge of God. The greatest need of the church in its present apostate environment is to reconnect with the Holy Spirit. [43]

You are the church. You are the one in danger of right now living in great deception. Are you really a Christian? Is your Christianity and relationship with God works oriented or an actual relationship with an actual God?

As I end this chapter, consider these verses from Mathew 7:21-27:

> "Not everyone that says unto me, Lord, Lord, shall enter into the kingdom of heaven; but he that does the will of my Father which is in heaven. Many will say to me in that day, Lord, Lord, have we not prophesied in your name? and in your name have cast out devils? and in your name done many wonderful works? And then will I profess unto them, I never knew you: depart from me, ye that work iniquity.

---

[43] For more information on the apostasy and the need for the Holy Spirit, check out my book, Revelation and the Age of the Antichrist.

Are We There Yet?

Therefore whosoever hears these sayings of mine, and does them, I will liken him unto a wise man, which built his house upon a rock: And the rain descended, and the floods came, and the winds blew, and beat upon that house; and it fell not: for it was founded upon a rock.

And every one that hears these sayings of mine, and does them not, shall be likened unto a foolish man, which built his house upon the sand: And the rain descended, and the floods came, and the winds blew, and beat upon that house; and it fell: and great was the fall of it."

The time is short. Apostasy rules. Let us stir up the Holy Spirit while He is still among us.

ARE WE THERE YET?

CHAPTER 2

Timeline 1
Toward the Last Days
Daniel 2

IN THE LAST CHAPTER, WE EXPLORED WHY THERE IS MUCH CONFUSION AND UNCERTAINITY SURROUNDING WHERE WE ARE ON GOD'S PROPHETIC/HISTORICAL timeline. In this chapter, we begin to look at the timelines recorded in the book of Daniel.

Our first timeline is found in Daniel 2. It lays the foundation for all timelines and last day events and outlines the main empires that rise and fall from the time of Nebuchadnezzar, king of Babylon, to the establishing of God's kingdom. Once this timeline is in place, all prophetic events and timelines can be placed in their proper time period.

Historically, Daniel's timeline has been confirmed as accurate. In hindsight we stand in amazement to how accurate Daniel's prophecy of future events is, as we now look at most of his future events as our past history; this gives to us the confidence that the unfulfilled prophecies will certainly take place as recorded. Daniel 2's timeline certainly qualifies as our starting point for ordering prophetic events.

A major hindrance to understanding the ordering of last day events is the lack of a single foundation on which prophetic events are built upon. Most do not have a problem understanding the events of the last days: apostasy, the Antichrist, great tribulation, rapture, and so forth, but are confused about how to order the events. Their confusion is the result of the different orderings that are used.

With such major differences, each cannot be right, and of course, everyone agrees with that. Nor are they all to be accepted as okay to hold onto, yet we accept the differences on the basis that "nobody really knows when prophetic events will take place." How can we content ourselves with this idea when Jesus revealed prophecy not as an exercise in philosophical ponderings, but to give certainty to keep us from being caught unaware and unprepared when the events take place?[44] Because of the vast differences, some students of prophecy have us presently in the great tribulation, some in the beginning of sorrows prior to the great tribulation; others have us in the trumpet judgments, while others have us in the seal judgments. Again, the reason for the differences is because no clear biblical timeline is used when understanding last day events.

If Daniel's timeline had been the starting point, there would be fewer contradictions when interpreting prophecy. We would then be able to build upon each other's efforts. As it is now, we have to relearn new approaches to the last days

---

[44] Matthew. 24:25, 32, 33; 1 Thessalonians 5:4-6.

Timeline 1: Toward the Last Days

depending on who we read. There should not be this much lack of unity within the church. Prophecy is not given so we can create our own scenarios. Prophecy is given so we can follow the scenarios already given.

Once we finish the end of this book, we will have outlined the end time scenarios through the timelines given in the books of Daniel, Matthew 24, and the book of Revelation. These are the keys to unlocking prophecy. We also will look at how the timelines in Daniel connects with the timeline in Matthew 24 and how Matthew's timeline connects with the timeline in the book of Revelation to reveal a comprehensive prophetic timeline.

Concerning timelines, they have a beginning and they have an end. All the events between the beginning and the end take place sequentially with the next event following the previous event. When we ask, "Has God given a prophetic/historical timeline?," we are asking if there is a timeline that doesn't need to be created and rearranged with a beginning, an ending, and events following sequentially from beginning to end without our rearranging? The answer is a booming—yes, and it begins with Daniel 2.

GOD ESTABLISHES EMPIRES

Before detailing the prophetic timeline, Daniel wanted there to be no misunderstanding to how empires are raised up and how they are removed from power. As much as we might like to think that presidents, kings, and empires rise and fall by the will or vote or military might of a government or its people, Daniel stresses that only God has this power:

ARE WE THERE YET?

> "Daniel answered and said, Blessed be the name of God forever and ever: for wisdom and might are his: And he changes the times and the seasons: he removes kings, and sets up kings: he gives wisdom unto the wise, and knowledge to them that know understanding."[45]

As we look with hindsight at the empires that have come to power, we understand that God most often removes world powers using the military of other nations. Though nation's like to think it was their superior might, they would not have had the victory if God did not give the permission. Jesus' statement to Pilate concerning Himself that, "You could have no power at all against me, except it were given you from above"[46] applies across the board with all of life. This also is stated in John 3:27 when "John answered and said, A man can receive nothing, except it be given him from heaven."

Nothing in this world takes place by chance. No one has power or authority that has not been given the okay by God. World War I, World War II, even the holocaust by Hitler did not happen only by the will of man. Even the world-wide influence of Elvis Presley, the Beatles, Dr. Spock, and Big Bird would not have been cultural changers if God had not permitted it. And what about the apostasy the church is going through and the increasing persecution against Christians? They would not be happening if God had not given His permission. God's permission does not mean God gives His blessing. As Romans 1:18-32 clearly points out, when people

---

[45] Daniel 2:20,21, 37; 5:21
[46] John 19:11

Timeline 1: Toward the Last Days

and nations continually reject God, eventually He lets them have what they want and the consequences that follow.

The nations recorded in our timelines are those that impact Israel. The nations that impact Israel determine the course of history. See Appendix A concerning Israel's role in prophecy. Throughout this book, we will find these nations are given their power and influence directly from the Devil to establish his body on earth to establish a world system that opposes God and God's people. It was Israel's rejection of God that launched the Devil's authority over the earth into high gear. He was given authority over the nations to develop his body on earth and a world in opposition to God, beginning with Babylon and king Nebuchadnezzar.

TIMELINE 1

After explaining to Nebuchadnezzar that the empires in his dream rise and fall only by the hand of God, Daniel then identifies the empires that would dominate the world throughout history, beginning with Babylon and ending with God's eternal kingdom.

Two of the empires, Babylon and Medes-Persia, were known to Daniel. One empire, the Grecian empire, was not a significant power when Daniel was alive and he may not have known it existed, except by name in his vision in chapter 8. The fourth empire was known by Daniel only as the "legs of iron" since the Roman Empire would have risen up much later after Daniel's death. Since these empires rise up in succession, we can safely conclude that the next empire to rise up after the Grecian would be the one history records as

ARE WE THERE YET?

the Roman Empire. There are those who suggest the Ottoman Empire is the "legs of iron," but it cannot be since it rose up much later and history is clear that it was the Romans who overcame the Grecian Empire. It is this unbroken succession that is important in Daniel 2's timeline.

These empires were also identified as parts of a body: Babylon the head of gold[47] and the Medes and Persians the breast and arms of silver that conquered Babylon.[48] The Medes and Persians were conquered by the Grecians, identified as the belly and thighs of brass.[49] These three were named by Daniel and confirmed by history. The Roman Empire is the longest lasting empire and is represented as the statue's legs.[50] The last empire is identified as the ten toes and is what we now call the New World Order, which is the realignment of all nations into ten political/economic regions.[51] This body is the body of the Devil on earth established to fulfill his will and to stand in opposition to the body of Christ.[52]

The nations represented are also seen in Revelation 12:3 and Revelation 13:1, 2. Here we are shown a great red dragon and a beast rising out of the sea. Both are described in the same way, showing they are the same beast pictured in different settings.

---

[47] Daniel 2:37, 38
[48] Daniel 2:32, 39; 5:28-31
[49] Daniel 2:32, 39
[50] Daniel 2:33, 40
[51] Daniel 2:33, 41
[52] See Appendix B concerning the Devil's will and agenda for earth as its god.

Timeline 1: Toward the Last Days

In Revelation 12:3 we are shown the Devil as he appeared in heaven:[53]

"And there appeared another wonder in heaven; and behold a great red dragon, having seven heads and ten horns, and seven crowns upon his heads."

In Revelation 13:1, 2, we are shown that when the dragon appears on earth he appears as particular empires,[54] identified here as a leopard, bear, and lion, the same empires identified in Daniel 7:

"And I stood upon the sand of the sea, and saw a beast rise up out of the sea, having seven heads and ten horns, and upon his horns ten crowns, and upon his heads the name of blasphemy. And the beast which I saw was like unto a leopard, and his feet were as the feet of a bear, and his mouth as the mouth of a lion: and the dragon gave him his power, and his seat, and great authority."

Note that in these passages the Devil is identified as a great red dragon and a beast having seven heads, ten horns, and ten crowns. Throughout Scripture a beast represents empires; heads represent nations; horns represent kings; and the crowns represent authority given to the kings over the nations.

Whereas Daniel sees these seven heads/empires after they were already in power, Revelation 13:1-2 reveal how they develop upon the earth as nations. Daniel 2 identified four of these empires as Babylon, Medes-Persia, the Grecian

---

[53] The dragon is identified as the Devil in Revelation 12:9
[54] The sea represents peoples, multitudes, nations, and languages as identified in Revelation 17:15.

ARE WE THERE YET?

Empire, and the Roman Empire. As we will see in Daniel 7, the last three empires are identified as a lion (Great Britain/United States), a bear (Russia), and Islam (the leopard). When these seven empires are merged as one composite empire in Revelation 13:2, they will be ruled by ten kings represented here as ten horns, and the ten toes of Daniel 2. It is this composite beast that forms the New World Order.

As much as we like to keep the Devil within the unseen air, we must be aware of his presence through the nations around us, whose goal is to create a society without the Creator God. Not recognizing his everyday, mundane influence upon our nations will keep us asleep to his real nature and keep us involved with his agenda.

In the chart below, the Devil's body is shown with its comparable empire. It also reveals a transfer of power from the Mideast (Babylon, Medes-Persia) to the West (Grecian, Roman Empires). As we will see in the next chapter, this power will return to the Mideast (Leopard Empire and 10 region new world order). All nations, East and West, will then assimilate into Islamic law, religion, culture, and government. Here is how Daniel relates the Devil's body to the empires in Daniel 2.

DEVIL'S BODY ON EARTH – DAN. 2

Head	Babylon	Dan. 2:32, 38
Shoulders/Arms	Medes/Persia	Dan. 2:32, 39
Belly/Thighs	Grecian	Dan. 2:32,
Legs	Roman	Dan. 2:33, 40
Ten Toes	NWO	Dan. 2:41-44

Timeline 1: Toward the Last Days

THE DIVIDED ROMAN EMPIRE

After falling from the height of its glory, the Roman Empire continued as a divided east and west empire as nation states. It is this divided empire today, lead by Great Britain and the United States, that leads all nations to the age of the Antichrist; yet this divided Roman Empire will not be the Antichrist's kingdom as many believe. As we will see later in this book, the divided Roman Empire becomes part of the Antichrist's ten-toed new world order.

It is this divided Roman Empire that is the driving force for moving the world toward a new global, cashless economic world order, identified in this first timeline as "ten toes." Because of its role in setting the stage for the Antichrist, many believe the Antichrist will come out of a revived Roman Empire. As we will discover throughout this book, that will not happen.

According to Daniel 2's timeline, located at the end of this chapter, we are currently living in this time of the divided Roman Empire. Looking at Daniel's timeline, Babylon, Medes-Persia, the Grecian, and the Roman empires have all risen to power and have fallen from the height of their power. Also, the ten-region new world order is now being established, but is not yet in place. This leaves us currently in the divided Roman Empire prior to the soon coming new world order (ten toes).

Daniel's timeline shows that we are the generation setting the stage for the appearance of the Antichrist. This means that we are the "this generation" of Matthew 24:34

ARE WE THERE YET?

that will see the rise of the final end time events, the Antichrist, and the return of Christ.

IN CLOSING

Our first timeline is the key to understanding where we are on the prophetic timeline. It is the first political/historical timeline recorded in Scripture and must be the timeline used to place all other timelines and prophetic events. It is this timeline that gives the overview of prophetic history from the time of Nebuchadnezzar, king of Babylon, to the coming of Christ and the end of the world. It is this timeline that will be used as our guide to place all timelines and prophetic events outlined in this book.

According to Daniel 2's timeline, we are now living in the time of the divided Roman Empire just prior to the coming to power of the global ten region new world order. We are the generation that is putting into place the last political, religious, and moral environment necessary for the Antichrist to arrive. Here is Timeline 1 from Daniel 2:

TIMELINE 1: Daniel 2

608 BC Babylon	Head	2:32, 37, 38
538 BC Medes-Persia	Breast/Arms	2:32, 39
333 BC Greece	Belly/Thighs	2:32, 39; 8:21
160 BC Rome	Legs of Iron	2:33, 40
476 AD Divided Rome	Legs of Iron	2:33, 41-43
20?? AD New World Order	Ten Toes	2:33, 41, 43
20?? AD God's Stone from Heaven		2:34, 44, 45

CHAPTER 3

Timeline 2
Toward The Final Years
Daniel 7

WITH DANIEL 2'S TIMELINE IN PLACE, THE NEXT TIMELINE CAN BE POSITIONED IN ITS PROPER TIME PERIOD. THIS TIMELINE IS FOUND IN DANIEL 7.

In Daniel 7's timeline, four new empires are introduced and identified as a lion, bear, and leopard (Dan. 7:3-7). To know where these empires fit into our first timeline, we need to determine when Daniel 7's empires rise upon the world stage. What we find is these empires are in power simultaneously and precede that time when the Antichrist arrives in power. We see this in Daniel 7:17-18 where God's people will take the kingdom from the Antichrist, which includes these animal empires. This happens only during the last seven years of earth's history when the Antichrist is in power. This places these empires in power immediately preceding the ten-toed empire during the time of the divided Roman Empire.

ARE WE THERE YET?

The following author sees this same last day setting (underline added):

> "Daniel knew only one thing about the rise of the four beasts, and that was, when the last beast was standing upon the great sea, the Lord would come to bring His Kingdom....The forces of Satan deceiving the nations, and preparing them to be drawn into the Middle East at the battle of Armageddon; the waves and the seas roaring; wars and rumors of wars; the major world powers' interest in the Mediterranean—<u>all these things would place the setting entirely in the last generation</u>. In fact, never in the history of the world until now have these four beasts been identifiable according to national emblems. However, all four beasts are very much in evidence today and all four are very much concerned about the Mediterranean Sea."[55]

The purpose of Daniel 7's empires is to set the stage for the Antichrist's arrival. We know this because these empires are the Devil's mouth, feet, and body. These are the parts of the body necessary to set the agenda (mouth), mobilize the body (feet), and give the form necessary for the mouth, feet, and heads to be connected to the body. This is revealed in Revelation 13:2 where we find a composite beast/empire with the mouth of a lion, the feet of a bear, and the body of a leopard. These are the same empires we find here in Daniel 7:3-7 (underline added):

> "And four great beasts came up from the sea, diverse one from another. The first was like a <u>lion</u>, and had <u>eagle's wings</u>: I beheld till the wings thereof were plucked, and it was lifted up from the earth, and made stand upon the

---

[55] Noah W. Hutchings, Daniel the Prophet, (Oklahoma City, OK: Hearthstone Publishing, 1998), 169-170.

Timeline 2: Toward the Final Years

feet as a man, and a man's heart was given to it. And behold another beast, a second, like to a bear, and it raised up itself on one side, and it had three ribs in the mouth of it between the teeth of it: and they said thus unto it, Arise, devour much flesh. After this I beheld, and lo another, like a leopard, which had upon the back of it four wings of a fowl; the beast had also four heads; and dominion was given to it.

After this I saw in the night visions, and behold a fourth beast, dreadful and terrible, and strong exceedingly; and it had great iron teeth: it devoured and broke in pieces, and stamped the residue with the feet of it: and it was diverse from all the beasts that were before it; and it had ten horns."

In Revelation 13:2 these same empires are shown connected to the body of the leopard:

"And the beast which I saw was like unto a leopard, and his feet were as the feet of a bear, and his mouth as the mouth of a lion: and the dragon gave him his power, and his seat, and great authority."

This composite beast has seven heads, which are the four empires of Daniel 2 and the three empires here in Daniel 7. We have already identified four of these empires in Daniel 2, and will identify the other three later in this chapter. These seven are: Babylon, Medes-Persia, Grecian, Roman, Great Britain/United States, Russia, and Islam.

Some have thought Daniel 7's empires were the same as those in Daniel 2. However, there are several reasons why these cannot be the same. Notice that Daniel did not have a clue to the identity of these four empires and asked one of

ARE WE THERE YET?

the angels near him to help him understand.[56] Also, if Daniel had related these empires to the ones in Daniel 2, as many commentators suggest, he would not have been so "grieved" and "troubled" trying to understand them, but he was.[57] Also, the angel explained these empires would "arise out of the earth."[58] The language here is that they were not presently upon the earth. If they were, they would not now be able to "rise up" if they had already done so. These empires would rise up much later after the rise and fall of the empires in Daniel 2.

We also know they will be on the world stage during earth's last seven years because "the saints of the most High shall take the kingdom, and possess the kingdom forever, even forever and ever."[59] This does not take place until the last seven years of earth's history[60] when the Antichrist is on the scene.

Also, Daniel 2 is clear that each successive empire overtook the one before it. Here in Daniel 7, the empires do not rise up overtaking each other, but are in power on the world scene at the same time. Daniel 7 does not identify any conflicts between them, only that they rise up in power from among its own people,[61] not from a people not of their empire.

---

56 Daniel 7:15,16
57 Daniel 7:15
58 Daniel 7:17
59 Daniel 7:18, 27
60 Daniel 7:7,8, 19-28
61 Daniel writes that these empires rise up out of the sea. The sea/waters represents peoples, languages, and nations according to Revelation 17:15. Therefore the conclusion is that Daniel 7's empires rise up from among the

Timeline 2: Toward the Final Years

Lastly, we know the animal symbol for the Grecian empire is the he-goat, while Medes-Persia is that of a Ram.[62] Daniel 7's empires are symbolized as a lion, eagle, bear, and leopard. There is no indication in Scripture or historically that these empires changed their animal identification.

WHO ARE THESE FINAL EMPIRES?

With the clues in the previous section, we know Daniel 7's empires:

1. Will rise up in the last of the last days
2. Will be in power at the same time
3. Will be great empires
4. Will rise up "out of the sea" (from among its own people)
5. Can be identified by the character of specific animals

Since we are presently living in Daniel's future and the last of the last days, these empires would now be on the world scene. To identify them, all we need to do is ask if there are four empires in power today that can be identified by the five clues listed above? If there are not, then Daniel's prophecy is not yet being fulfilled. If the answer is yes, we can conclude we are living in the time of their fulfillment. The answer is an astonishing yes...here's why.

---

people of that empire and not from being overtaken or conquered by a foreign people.
62 Daniel 8:20,21

ARE WE THERE YET?

For the first time in world history, three of the four empires are now in full power on the world stage and the fourth is presently rising up. There have been nations throughout history that have identified with the animals of Daniel 7, but never at any time in history have four great empires ruled on the world stage at the same time with these characteristics... not until now.

Without question, Great Britain is the lion, the United States the eagle, which separated from the lion, and Russia is the bear, even taking these as their national animals. Each of these are indisputable. Each are empires and dominate players on the world stage at the same time. Each also became world powers developing "from among its people"[63] and not from being overtaken by another nation. And each are presently on the world stage to sit in place and lead the world to the new world order government of the Antichrist.

Not as indisputable is who the leopard empire is. Though no great empire has yet claimed the leopard as its national animal, there are a people rising up right now with the characteristics of the leopard, with considerable influence affecting world affairs, and developing into a great empire...and that is the Islamic people.

The character of Islam is much like that of the leopard. Like the leopard, Islam's fighters prefer to work, fight, and live alone, avoiding living or traveling in groups. A leopard will live concealed among its prey, hiding its real intentions by assimilating into its surroundings. It uses the element of

---

[63] Daniel 7:3. Sea represents "peoples, and multitudes, and nations, and tongues" (Revelation 17:15).

Timeline 2: Toward the Final Years

surprise, not letting its prey know it is being stalked. When it does attack, it does so quickly and without warning. Even the color of the leopard, tan with black spots, no doubt represents the tan Middle Eastern and the black African Islamists

Here's how another author describes the leopard: [64]

> "The leopard is a ferocious beast and relatively small in comparison to a bear or lion. According to Jeremiah 5:6 and Hosea 13:7, we know they stalk their prey. While the nature of a lion is of a kingly bearing, protective toward its family, methodical in its hunting habits, and reticent to attack either man or other wild beasts except when it is hungry or its domain is threatened, the characteristics of the third Mediterranean power is strikingly different from either the lion or the bear. The leopard is a cunning animal with seemingly no self protective instincts. It is one of the few animals in the world that will attack a man without provocation."

Because the other three empires are presently in power, and Islam is presently rising up with great influence with the character of our five clues above, Islam is without question the leopard empire. If the other three empires were not on the world stage, Islam would not be a consideration, but since they are, Islam is destined to establish the environment for advancing the new world order of the fourth, ten-toed final empire.

This leopard is unique from the other beasts in that it has four wings. It also has four heads representing a coalition

---

[64] Noah W. Hutchings, Daniel the Prophet, (Oklahoma City, OK: Hearthstone Publishing, 1998), 176-177.

ARE WE THERE YET?

of nations and may be the Islamic nations of Iraq, Iran, Libya, and Syria. These are continually in the news and are presently major influencers on the world scene. The four wings represent four political ideologies. Unlike the United States (two eagle wings on the lion) whose political ideologies led them to break away from Great Britain, the leopard's wings remain attached, indicating the ideologies remain unified with the leopard.

Now that the leopard is presently rising up, it is working hard to lead the world to the age of the Antichrist through terror, assimilation, immigration, and the changing of local and national laws to conform to Sharia law. Ever wonder why thousands of Muslims are immigrating to Europe, America, and Russia? Ever wonder why Islam seeks to terrorize and live in cities and countries throughout the world without assimilating into the culture of its host country? Ever wonder why you hear of America becoming an Islamic nation? Have you ever wondered why some churches embrace Islam? Now you know.

The chart below shows how the Devil's body on earth now looks when added to the body parts of Daniel 2. Note that the mouth, feet, and flesh complete the body's formation and are the parts necessary to give vision and to mobilize the vision. As we will see throughout this chapter, these empires are presently upon the earth. We are now in position for the development of the ten-toed, new world order fourth beast to develop out from the feet. Here's how the Devil's body looks in chart form:

Timeline 2: Toward the Final Years

DEVIL'S BODY ON EARTH

Head	Babylon	2:32, 38
Shoulders/Arms	Medes/Persia	2:32, 39
Belly/Thighs	Grecian	2:32,
Legs	Roman	2:33, 40
Voice	Great Britain	7:4, Rev 13:2
Voice	United States	7:4, Rev 13:2
Feet	Russia	7:5, Rev 13:2
Body	Islam	7:6, Rev 13:2
Ten Toes	NWO	2:41-44, 7:7,8

AMERICA'S PROPHETIC DESTINY

Concerning America's prophetic destiny, Scripture identifies America's role as the mouth/voice of the new world order to lead and set in place the global environment necessary for the cashless society, new world order global governance, and rise of the Antichrist.

How this is played out in today's world is clearly seen after being hidden in plain sight since America's beginnings, until recent decades. It is now clearly understood that America was never established to be a Christian nation, but to lead the world toward the age of the Antichrist.

This destiny was designed more than one hundred fifty years before the American Revolution—before America became an independent nation—by Sir Francis Bacon in the early 1600's. He was convinced that the New World (America) was to be the New Atlantis and set in motion plans to see his ideas come to life. Much of his vision for the New

ARE WE THERE YET?

Atlantis came from Plato's description of the lost Atlantis in his books, the *Critias* and *Timaeus*.

Details of America's true destiny, and how it has been moving steadily from America's beginnings toward Bacon's ideal, may be found in the writings of Manly P. Hall, James Wasserman, and Robert Hieronimus.

Manly P. Hall outlines how the plans for the founding of America began one thousand years before the beginning of the Christian era and was put into action during the colonial age. The plan involved America ushering the world toward what today is called the new world order.[65]

James Wasserman reveals the meaning of the symbolism hidden throughout Washington D.C. from its design, monuments, structures, etc. in dedication to the forces that moves our nation to set the stage for the arrival of the Antichrist and the new world order.[66]

Robert Hieronimus shows how the majority of the Founding Fathers were not involved with establishing our nation as a Christian nation, but one that paves the way for the new world order and the Antichrist.[67]

In our twenty-first century, what was once seen as the fanatical ravings of conspiracy theorists are now everyday headlines and on the lips of world leaders. Movement toward a cashless society is a reality and gaining momentum. Hope

---

[65] Manly P. Hall, The Secret Destiny of America (New York, NY; Penguin Group, 2008).
[66] James Wasserman, The Secrets of Masonic Washington (Rochester, VT; Destiny Books, 2008).
[67] Robert Hieronimus, PHD. Founding Fathers, Secret Societies (Rochester, VT; Destiny Books, 2006).

Timeline 2: Toward the Final Years

for our world through world governance continues to occupy the time of political meetings. The need for someone, anyone, any entity to lead—whether they be man, God, or Devil, is a great yearning. These events are so real and so close that you and I could wake up one morning to a world that is quite different from the one we knew the night before.

RUSSIA'S PROPHETIC ROLE

The feet of this composite, new world order beast are that of a bear. The main purpose of feet is to mobilize the body and to assist in standing and balance. Through its various alliances with Islamic nations, Russia gives the stability and mobility to its Islamic neighbors that will support them in coming against Israel.[68] This is represented with the feet/Russia being attached to the body of the leopard/Islam.

Russia is in a unique position to form strong alliances in the Middle East, while maintaining open communication with the West. They are very much a Middle Eastern country with a land mass extending over the whole of Northern Asia and forty percent of Europe, making it by land mass very much a Middle Eastern country. Yet its people, culture, large cities, and political institutions are mostly western, following the European model. With its mix of European and Asian, it cannot rightly be called either a European or Asian country. Due to this unique position, Russia must always be in tune to its Middle Eastern people as well as its European population.

---

[68] Ezekiel 38-39

ARE WE THERE YET?

Russia's position allows this bear to be the key instrument in transferring world power back to the Middle-East in the same way the Grecian Empire was instrumental in transferring world power to the West.

THE FOURTH BEAST

After Great Britain, the United States, Russia, and Islam are on the world stage at the same time, Daniel then identifies a fourth brutal beast[69] as the final empire that rises up to usher in the last seven years of earth's history with the Antichrist as its ruler. This beast appears out of the leopard empire. We know this because this fourth beast is also the composite beast of Revelation 13:2 and its body is that of the leopard:

> "And the beast which I saw was like unto a leopard, and his feet were as the feet of a bear, and his mouth as the mouth of a lion: and the dragon gave him his power, and his seat, and great authority."

The body of this beast is Islam (the leopard). Its voice/mouth is that of a lion. Great Britain is this lion, with the United States, giving leadership to lead the world to set in place the Antichrist's new world order. Great Britain and the United States' leadership in the world are without question.

The purpose of this fourth beast is the total removal of Israel and all of God's people from off the face of the earth. Once thought impossible, we are presently seeing a scenario of Great Britain, America, Russia, and the Islamic nations

---

[69] Daniel 7:7

Timeline 2: Toward the Final Years

increasingly working and moving in concert toward similar goals in what is called the new world order, which also involves positioning Islam to control the nations.

Concerning America's support of Islam, America has supported Islam through the years in order to advance her cause.[70] According to the Scripture we've looked at, America has been raised up, with Great Britain, to lead the world to the Antichrist's new world order and its final destiny to attach itself to the Antichrist's Islamic body.

Here's another unsettling thought for those who take pride in holding on to what we call America's "Christian" heritage. Who gave Great Britain, the United States, Russia, and Islam its power and authority to act? Look at the last part of Revelation 13:2:

> "And the dragon gave him his power, and his seat, and great authority."

It is the dragon/Devil that gives the power to the beast and the empires attached to it to exert his will over the entire earth; and it is God who gives the Devil the authority, as the god of this world, to raise up these empires, not for a righteous, godly purpose, but for his own. In this light, the United States was never established for Christian purposes. Ever wonder how a nation with the majority of its population identified as Christian could become so hedonistic that it

---

[70] A couple of books that speak of America's support to Islam are: Rabbi, Menachem Kohen, Prophecies For The Era of Muslim Terror (Brooklyn, NY: Lambda Publishers, Inc. 2007), 82-87; and Robert Dreyfuss, Devil's Game: How the United States Helped Unleash Fundamentalist Islam (New York, NY: Metropolitan Books, 2006).

ARE WE THERE YET?

sacrifices thousands of babies each year, creates an educational system opposed to God, trusts in politics and the legal system above God, and continues to remove Christianity from its culture? The apostasy of our present age is much greater than most of us are willing to admit.

THE NEW WORLD ORDER

The composite beast of Revelation 13, which is the same as Daniel's fourth beast and ten toed empire, is the empire world leaders are presently moving the nations toward when they speak of the new world order. This new world order is the realignment of all nations into ten economic/political regions. Plans for this realignment came into public focus with the release of the report, *Regionalized and Adaptive Model of the Global World System* in September 1973 by the Club of Rome, an organization created in 1968 and given the responsibility to oversee the regionalization and unification of all nations. Their members consist of "notable scientists, economists, businessmen, high level civil servants and former heads of state from around the world."[71] Their goal is to advance a global government. In their report they revealed the dividing of the world into ten political/economic regions; the map below shows these regions.

---

71 www.clubofrome.org/about-us

Timeline 2: Toward the Final Years

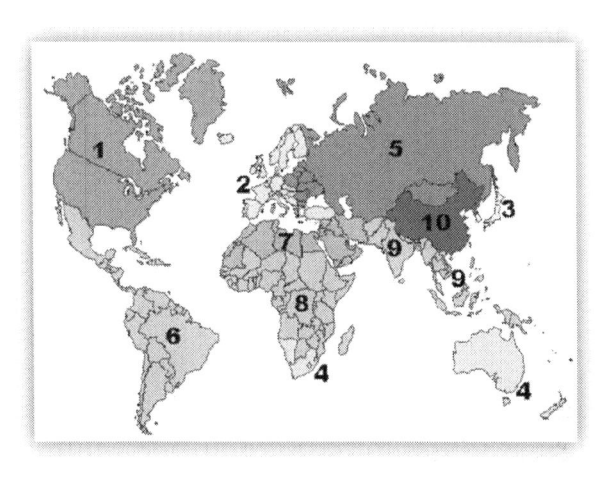

The Club of Rome's plan is not isolated to this group. The United Nations also has outlined ten Regional Groupings on page 55 of its report, *The Millennium Development Goals Report 2009*. These geographical groupings are used as they seek to maintain international peace and security, promote sustainable global development, and uphold international law. The bottom line is, the United Nations is becoming a global government with the nations gradually giving up their sovereignty to them. Here's the map from the United Nation's report:[72]

---

[72] The regional groupings in this report are identified as Developed Regions, Countries of the Commonwealth of Independent States (CIS), Northern Africa, sub-Saharan Africa, South-Eastern Asia, Oceana, Eastern Asia, Southern Asia, Western Asia, and Latin America and the Caribbean.

ARE WE THERE YET?

Regional Groupings map showing developed regions, Countries of the Commonwealth of Independent States (CIS), Northern Africa, Sub-Saharan Africa, South-Eastern Asia, Oceania, Eastern Asia, Southern Asia, Western Asia, Latin America & the Caribbean.

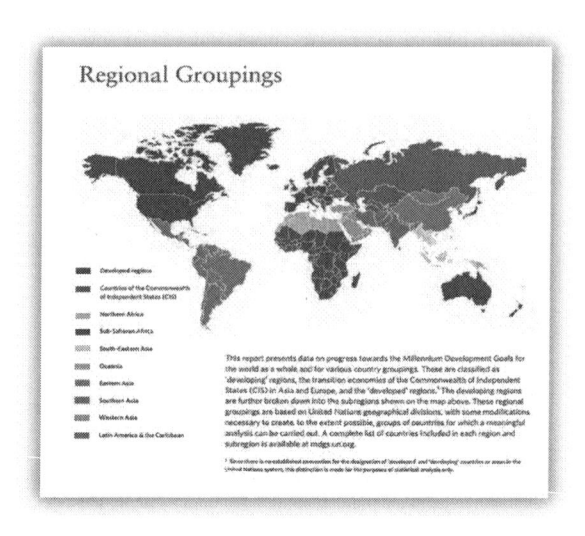

The United Nations was founded in 1945 to help deal with international issues and advance a global government. Today it is increasingly receiving power and authority to act on behalf of nations. Eventually the ten region realignment of all nations will most likely take place through the United Nations. Once in place, the Antichrist will then take up the leadership.

These regional groupings by the Club of Rome and the United Nations reveal that the arrival of the ten region political/economic fourth beast is no longer in our far distant future, but is already implemented in the thinking and policies of world leaders. It is so close that we could wake-up one morning to find that the world we have known has drastically changed.

A major catalysts for uniting all nations into ten regions is the ushering in of a cashless society. Once the cashless

Timeline 2: Toward the Final Years

economic system is in place and ready to roll, then the realignment of governments and economies under these regions will take place. It is the role of Islam to prepare the instability needed to give the nations cause for giving up their sovereignty in the name of world peace, financial stability, and global security.

This realignment will be in place before the Antichrist takes leadership. World leaders speak of this realignment using variations of the term, "new world order." Pay attention to how variations of this term are used and how frequent. This term will let us know how close we are to the formation of the soon coming economic/political realignment.

THE ANTICHRIST TAKES CONTROL

Soon after the new world order is formed, the Antichrist will take over its leadership as outlined in Daniel 7:7, 8, 20, 24. It is this global realignment that makes this beast different from any other empire throughout history. The basis for the restructuring is economic, forcing everyone to submit to it in order to buy or sell anything. That our world is moving toward this direction is now a reality, summarized in these statements by financial analysts:

> "The movement toward electronic money is moving at high speed and this says a lot about the state of the financial system."[73]

---

[73] www.washingtonsblog.com/ Why The Powers That Be Are Pushing A Cashless Society May 4, 2015 by Washingtons Blog

ARE WE THERE YET?

> "Administration of world money and world taxation will be conducted by world government. Most of this architecture is already in place."[74]

The ten horns of Daniel's fourth beast represent the ten kings who will rule over this realignment of nations. [75] It will be out of this new order of nations that the little horn (king) will appear. He is the one we call the Antichrist. When he comes to power, he will remove three of the ten kings. These kings will then be given the authority to blaspheme God and persecute and kill God's people throughout their particular region.[76] This global holocaust is the great tribulation.

Though this man, the Antichrist, will appear to be a man, he will speak as a god and come in the power of the Devil on earth.[77] He will be given authority to exert his destructive will for a short three and a half years. His kingdom will then be taken from him, returned to God, and he will be thrown into the lake of fire.[78]

The Antichrist's kingdom is described as a terrifying beast and not a specific animal since it is a composite of many beasts/empires. It is truly a global empire with the goal and power to brutally destroy God's people. It is exceedingly strong, dreadful, and terrible with teeth as iron that can devour and crush as it pleases. So terrifying is this beast that, after devouring and crushing its opponents, it then tramples

---

74 Jim Rickards, "The Power Elite's Plan for You and the Entire World." Laissez Faire Letter, April 2016, Volume 3, Issue 7.
75 Daniel 7:24; Revelation 17:12
76 Daniel 7:8,20,21,25
77 Daniel 7:7,8
78 Revelation 19:20

Timeline 2: Toward the Final Years

and pulverizes them with his feet. In my book, *Revelation and the Age of the Antichrist,* I make the following observation:[79]

> "This beast completes the path for the Antichrist to appear. This beast is different from the previous empires with more cruelty and brutality in the advancement of its goals. This beast is the same composite beast in Revelation 13:2. It appears the Islamic State, formerly named ISIL and ISIS, may be this fourth beast in its development stage. If it is, when this beast reaches maturity, the new world order and the Antichrist will appear. The brutality of this fourth beast is described in Daniel 7 with these adjectives: teeth of iron, nails of brass, devour, break in pieces, and stamping of the residue with his feet. These adjectives also describe the Islamic State. The group's acts of brutality are so cruel that other terrorist groups, including al-Qaeda, have condemned and distanced themselves from them, as the following author observed:
>
> "And after al-Qaeda rejected AQI because of tactics such as this, tactics so depraved and brutal that they even repulsed al-Qaeda leader Osama bin Laden, what did AQI become?
> The Islamic State of Iraq and Syria.
> It became ISIS."

ISIS became the Islamic State (IS) and will eventually evolve into this fourth, terrifying, Antichrist Empire. The stage is now being set. It won't be long.

Pay close attention to the development of the Islamic State throughout the world. They are another marker on how close we are to the arrival of the Antichrist. The more they

---

[79] Steve Magill, Revelation and the Age of the Antichrist. (Enumclaw, WA: Redemption Press, 2015). 61-62

immigrate...the more they terrorize...the more they control... the closer we are to earth's final years.

WHEN DOES THE ANTICHRIST APPEAR?

There is much speculation about when the Antichrist will appear. Every generation has speculated that he was on the scene and ready to make his appearance. When the prophetic timeline is followed, much speculation can be set aside as it reveals specific events that must take place before the man of sin, the son of the Devil,[80] appears. Understanding the prophetic timeline, we have assurance of how close we are to his appearing. Daniel 8 records that the Antichrist appears "at the time of the end shall be the vision."[81]

The "time of the end" refers to the end of desolations and God's judgment on Israel during the seventieth week of the seventy weeks when the Antichrist brings about the global holocaust of God's people. This also is referred to as the end of the indignation in Daniel 8:19.

The indignation is the same event as the desolation and is that time when God's fury and anger are released upon the world at large and upon His people specifically through the event called the great tribulation. It began to move toward this end when the last days began with the appearance of Jesus. Jesus spoke of the events that would continually increase until reaching the very end of the indignation when they would then culminate with the Antichrist and the horrors he will release upon the earth. The Antichrist

---

80 2 Thessalonians 2:3; John 17:12
81 Daniel 8:17

Timeline 2: Toward the Final Years

appears when God's indignation against sin comes to its end during the last seven years of earth's history.

The indignation will continue until the times of the gentiles are fulfilled, as recorded in Luke 21:24:

> "And they shall fall by the edge of the sword, and shall be led away captive into all nations: and Jerusalem shall be trodden down of the Gentiles, until the times of the Gentiles be fulfilled."

When the times of the gentiles have reached their peak, the Antichrist will rise up to complete the indignation and desolation of Israel.[82] We know the times of the gentiles are ending and the Antichrist will soon arrive because Israel has returned as a nation and has gained control over Jerusalem as her capital. These are key signposts of last day events, signaling the beginning of the last generation, the "this generation" of Matthew 24 that will usher the world into earth's last seven years.

In order for the Antichrist (the abomination of desolation) to confirm a peace treaty with Israel and establish himself in the temple, Israel had to return as a sovereign nation and regain Jerusalem as her capital. Once the Antichrist sets himself up in the temple, he will complete the times of the Gentiles by ushering Israel and all God's people into the great tribulation, and once again trample under foot Jerusalem.[83] After Jesus returns to the earth,

---

82 Daniel 8:23
83 Revelation 11:1,2

destroys the Antichrist, and establishes his millennium kingdom, the times of the gentiles will be complete.

The times of the gentiles are the times when sin is permitted to increase, the gentiles are given the opportunity to receive the inheritance given to Abraham, and Jerusalem would be under gentile control. Gentile rule over Jerusalem began to end in 1967 when Israel recaptured it during the Six-Day War, claiming it again as its capital. This event is the key event signaling that we have entered the last of the last days and the age of the Antichrist. This event is the key event signaling we have entered the "this generation" of Matthew 24:34.

THIS GENERATION SHALL NOT PASS

The last of the last days is referred to when Jesus taught, "This generation shall not pass, till all these things be fulfilled."[84] The generation that sees the fulfillment of Matthew 24's events, and the rise of the Antichrist, would be the generation that witnesses earth's last seven years and the return of Christ.

A generation is the normal life span given to a person, which is seventy years.[85] Seventy years added to the year Israel regained control over Jerusalem would bring the timeframe for the fulfillment of prophetic events between 1967 and 2037. Israel's control of Jerusalem is used as the beginning of the "this generation" because it signals the beginning of the end of gentile control over Jerusalem and

---

[84] Matthew 24:34
[85] Psalm 90:10

Timeline 2: Toward the Final Years

the beginning to the end of Israel's desolation and God's indignation on them. This time frame doesn't mean we have until 2037, but that at some point within this time frame the final events will be complete, the Antichrist will arrive, and Jesus will return.

As of this writing, we know the earth has more than seven years before our present age ends. There will be three and one-half years of peace with Israel due to a confirming of a treaty with them for seven years. After three and one-half years, the treaty will be broken and the great tribulation by the Antichrist will take place for three and one-half years. After the great tribulation, Christ returns, the rapture takes place, and God releases His final hour of wrath.

After the Antichrist arrives, he mandates his global economic system with the mark of the beast and ushers in the great tribulation. When he is on the scene, we then know there are only seven years left to our present age. Here's how this looks in chart form:

EARTH'S FINAL 7 YEARS		
7 Year Treaty Confirmed		**God's Hour of Wrath**
Treaty Signed	**Treaty Broken**	**Christ Returns** **Rapture Takes Place**
3 ½ Years of Peace	3 ½ Years of Tribulation	**Hour of God's Wrath**
	7 Seals Unleashed 7 Trumpets Sounds	7 Vials Poured Out

ARE WE THERE YET?

Having said this, let's revisit Psalm 90:10:

> "The days of our years are threescore years and ten; and if by reason of strength they be fourscore years, yet is their strength labor and sorrow; for it is soon cut off, and we fly away."

Note that the seventy-year limitation to a generation has some flexibility. If a person has good health, they could live to be eighty or longer. It seems the arrival of Antichrist could be delayed, but only within the time span allotted one generation. Once the Antichrist is in power, no delay is possible and the countdown to earth's final years begins.

Do I think it's *probable* that we could go beyond 2037? No, I think we are long passed the possibility of repentance. Do I think it's *possible* that we could go beyond 2037? Yes, but it would take a miracle, and that miracle is dependent on God's people returning to relationship with Him.

As I consider what the world will be like prior to the Antichrist's arrival, I don't think it matters much whether we have a delay or not. The important thing is to be ready. Have you repented of your sins? Do you know Jesus Christ?

WHERE DOES THE ANTICHRIST COME FROM?

The question of where the Antichrist comes from is answered in Daniel 8. This chapter begins with Medes-Persia, represented as "a ram which had two horns"[86] who goes to war with a "he goat from the west."[87] Daniel 8 records that

---

[86] Daniel 8:3, 20
[87] Daniel 8:5, 21

Timeline 2: Toward the Final Years

the "he-goat" is the Grecian Empire.[88] Commentators and historians agree that this refers to Alexander the Great who defeated Medes-Persia.

Alexander's empire became great and while it was strong and Alexander was still young, he died. It was then that his empire was divided among his four generals:[89] Ptolemy I ruled over the Southern part of the kingdom in Egypt; Cassendar ruled over the Western part of the kingdom which included Greece, the South Eastern part, and Thrace; Seleucus ruled most of Asia Minor and the Middle East in the North, which included Babylon, Persia, Syria, Mesopatamia, and surrounding areas; and Eastern Asia Minor, which includes Western Turkey, was ruled by Lysimachis

Daniel 8:9 is clear that out of one of these divisions a "little horn" rises up. Commentators agree that this "little horn" is the one called the Antichrist. We know he rises out of the Northern kingdom since Daniel 8:9 records that his great military exploits takes him to the South, East, and West, which leaves the Northern kingdom as his starting point.

We also know this "little horn" is the Antichrist because Daniel 8:10 records that he has the power to grow so great that even the host of heaven and angels are cast down and trampled on by him. No earthly ruler has had this power, only the one with the power of the Devil, who is also known as the "son of the Devil," the Antichrist.[90]

---

88 Daniel 8:21
89 Daniel 8:8
90 2 Thessalonians 2:3; Genesis 3:15

ARE WE THERE YET?

Daniel 11 also confirms that the Antichrist arrives out of the Northern division of Alexander's kingdom, identified here as coming out of Syria, which is part of Seleucus' division. That the Antichrist will be Syrian is also recorded by the prophets Isaiah and Micah.[91]

Daniel 11 records ongoing conflict throughout history between the king of the North (Syria) and the king of the South (Egypt). Daniel 11 records that the Antichrist will arrive as the last Northern king. See Appendix C for a brief historical commentary on Daniel 11. Following this chronology, the last Northern King would be Syrian. Most commentaries agree this last king is the Antichrist; therefore, that would also make him a Syrian coming out of Syria.

MORE THAN A MAN

Daniel 8:10 reveals that this one we call the Antichrist is more than a man. No man has ever trampled on and cast down the angels of heaven. Only the Devil and his angels could have access to the angels and to Michael the archangel, identified as "the Prince of the hosts."[92] In my book, *Revelation and the Age of the Antichrist,* I reveal the Antichrist to be a fallen angel.

This great host of fallen angels is released to the Antichrist for the purpose of removing the daily sacrifices—an event brought on because of Israel's sin[93]—to disregard truth, and to fulfill the Devil's will to engage God's people in

---

[91] Micah 5:5; Isaiah 10:24, 14:25
[92] Daniel 8:11
[93] Daniel 8:11,12

Timeline 2: Toward the Final Years

all out war to complete God's indignation and desolation on Israel.[94] Daniel 2:43 also indicates fallen angels will be with the Antichrist:

> "And whereas you saw iron mixed with miry clay, they shall mingle themselves with the seed of men: but they shall not cleave one to another, even as iron is not mixed with clay."

Note the fact that "they" will "mingle with the seed of men." The "they" in this verse distinguishes itself from "the seed of men." We know the "seed" is the life giving force of a man and refers to man. The "they" is distinguished here as being something not of the race of man. These are the fallen angels whom God cast out of heaven into the earth along with the Devil in Revelation 12:4, 7-9. Apparently, the Devil and his angels are not able to function on the earth in the same way people do, therefore making it necessary for them to create human bodies compatible to their own spirit-form. Just as God became flesh to defeat the Devil, the Devil and his angels also need to become flesh in their attempt to steal the inheritance from Christ and His people.

Even as God merged His Spirit with man's DNA to become flesh,[95] so must the fallen angels do the same.[96] At first glance, it appears in Daniel 2:43 that the fallen angels procreated with women in the same way that men do, and it's possible that, after creating a body for themselves, they

---

94 Daniel 8:11-24
95 2 Corinthians 5:19
96 Angels are presently spirits (Hebrews 1:14)

were able to do that, but Daniel indicates before they got to that point, they had to merge their DNA with the seed and DNA of man. Once they were able to mingle with man's seed, they were then able to create bodies allowing them to appear on the earth with the substance of a person.

Angels are a totally different creature than man and cannot procreate with humans. In the same way that dogs cannot breed with cats, or horses breed with deer, neither can angels breed with people. Each species is species specific to their own kind. Therefore, these fallen angels must manipulate DNA, the building blocks that make a living creature, in order to make it compatible with their spirit-form. That they would have knowledge of this process is indicated in Psalm 139:15, a verse I find absolutely incredible:

> "My substance was not hid from you, when I was made in secret, and curiously formed in the lowest parts of the earth."

The implication is that we were created somewhere in the lower parts of this physical earth, and then placed in the womb when the seed of man combined with the egg of a woman. The angels would have been involved with this process and had knowledge of how to do it. This is seen in Genesis 1:26 when God said, "Let us make man in our image," which refers to God speaking to the angels.

The angel's difficulty now is not having access to the materials to make it happen. Since they no longer have access to anything that is in the house and kingdom of God, they are dependent on what is already created: men, women, children,

Timeline 2: Toward the Final Years

and animals. One of the chief characteristics of what is known as alien abduction is the manipulations and surgeries that have to do with the internal and external sexual anatomy of the person abducted.[97]

As I speak briefly in the next section, what are known as UFO's are actually fallen angels. After God created these angels, no new ones were created. What appears to be going on now is not the bringing forth of an entity that does not exist, but the creation of a body for a spirit entity that already exists.

Daniel 2:43 is clear that this angel/man combination does not work out when Daniel writes: "They shall not cleave one to another."

One of the consequences of this incompatibility is the permeating of every cell of this angel/man hybrid with sin and violence as it was in the days of Noah when the fallen angels first merged with people.[98] Since there would be no living soul in the angel/human hybrid—seeing as the "living soul" is the Spirit of God[99]—there would be no characteristics of God's Spirit: love, joy, peace, patience, gentleness, goodness, faith, meekness, or self-control.[100]

How many fallen angels are there that need bodies to walk upon the earth? It is recorded that when Lucifer fell from heaven he caused one third of the angels in heaven to

---

[97] David Ruffino, Unholy Communion (Crane, MO: Defender Publishing House).
98 Genesis 6:5; Genesis 6:11
99 Genesis 2:7
100 Galatians 5:22, 23

ARE WE THERE YET?

fall with him.[101] Scripture is clear there are at least one hundred million angels,[102] and that number is extremely low considering Scripture also records that the angels are innumerable.[103] One third of one hundred million is approximately thirty-three million fallen angels. Imagine having thirty-three million fallen angels walking the earth with the ultimate goal of ruling over us. Talk about an invasion by a hostile alien force—it is coming. No wonder Daniel became sick and the Apostle John became violently sick when they understood what was coming to the earth and God's people in the last days.[104]

Revelation 12:9 informs us that the Devil and his angels are cast "into" the earth. "Into" indicates they were sent into the interior of the earth, under the mountains and seas, after being cast out of their heavenly habitation. They are now here, actively engaged in preparing bodies for themselves in order to rule the earth and destroy God's people. Many angel/human hybrids are walking among us even now. Check out my book, *Revelation and the Age of the Antichrist,* for more information on the fallen angels living within the interior of our earth.

---

[101] Revelation 12:4
[102] Revelation 12:11: And I beheld, and I heard the voice of many angels round about the throne and the beasts and the elders: and the number of them was ten thousand times ten thousand, and thousands of thousands; See also Daniel 7:10; Hebrews 12:22; Revelation 5:11.
[103] Hebrews 12:22
[104] Daniel 8:27; Revelation 10:9-10

Timeline 2: Toward the Final Years

THEY ARE HERE!

In Revelation 12:7-9, the Apostle John is shown that the Devil and his angels are removed from heaven and enter into the earth because of a battle that took place in heaven between Michael and his angels and the Devil and his angels:

> "And there was war in heaven: Michael and his angels fought against the dragon; and the dragon fought and his angels, And prevailed not; neither was their place found any more in heaven. And the great dragon was cast out, that old serpent, called the Devil, and Satan, which deceives the whole world: he was cast out into the earth, and his angels were cast out with him."

According to Revelation 12's chronology, the Devil and his angels entered *into* the earth after Christ ascended to the right hand of God, Israel was scattered into all nations, and then reformed as a sovereign nation. This would date the Devil's entrance *into* the earth around 1948 when Israel reformed as a sovereign nation. Since Israel has now regained its statehood, we also know the fallen angels are now with us. The trillion-dollar question is: where are they now?

Since we know the fallen angels entered *into* the earth around the time Israel returned as a nation in May 1948, we only need to ask if there is any evidence of their appearance on earth around that time? There is, through what is known as the UFO phenomenon. In a CIA report, it was stated,[105]

---

[105] Gerald K. Haines, "CIA's Role in the Study of UFO's, 1947-1990" (cia.gov/library/center-for-the-study-of-intelligence).

ARE WE THERE YET?

> "The first report of a 'flying saucer' over the United States came on 24 June 1947, when Kenneth Arnold, a private pilot and reputable businessman, while looking for a downed plane sighted nine disk-shaped objects near Mt. Rainier, Washington, traveling at an estimated speed of over 1,000 mph. Arnold's report was followed by a flood of additional sightings, including reports from military and civilian pilots and air traffic controllers all over the United States."

Another report, by the University of Arizona in 1967, made this observation:

> "The Report on the UFO Wave of 1947 discusses the first contemporary wave of UFO sightings in this country, which reached its peak on July 6-7, 1947. It includes a detailed chronology of more than 850 UFO cases for June and July with complete references, primarily from 140 newspapers in 90 cities in the United States and Canada, but also from the files of NICAP and Project Blue Book, as well as references from a number of publications on UFOs."[106]

The amazing fact about these first sightings is that they were not influenced by previous sightings—there were none. Neither were they inspired by the latest UFO movie or newspaper article—there were none. These sightings took place because they were experienced by the observer without previous knowledge of what they could be.

These UFO sightings appearing after the battle between Michael and the Devil in heaven and Israel becoming a nation

---

[106] Ted Bloecher, "Report on the UFO Wave of 1947" (University of Arizona: 1967).

Timeline 2: Toward the Final Years

again is more than a coincidence. There is no doubt in this author's mind that what we call UFO's are the fallen angels who were cast out of heaven to live within the earth.

Another author reported that UFO's drastically increased from 277 reported sightings in 1990 to 7086 reported sightings in 2013.[107] This increase in activity is the increase of fallen angels as they shape the world to receive the realignment of all nations into ten political/economic regions and the age of the Antichrist.

It is interesting that it was after 1948 that we've witnessed an exponential increase in travel, knowledge, technology, and opposition to Christ and Christianity—no doubt consequences of the fallen angels influencing the world's course. How could they do this without being detected? Angels throughout the Bible are no different in looks than men and walk among us without our being aware of them.[108]

What has been identified as UFO's has been seen throughout man's history. However, before these sightings in 1947, they were rarely seen. After 1947, they have been seen by the hundreds and sightings are now commonplace. Massive sightings and sightings by groups of people are also more frequent and open. Apparently, they are now secretly preparing for a very real, physical conflict with man when God's people will be persecuted and killed during the great

---

[107] Richard M. Dolan, UFOs for the 21st Century Mind (Rochester, NY: Richard Dolan Press 2014), 356.
[108] Hebrews 13:2

tribulation and the nations will be influenced to come against God at the battle of Armageddon.

As believers, the inheritance we will receive is far greater than any hardships the world may throw at us. Discerning this reality will keep us from giving in to the pressure during the perilous age of the Antichrist. Concerning this concept, the Apostle Paul wrote in Romans 8:18:

> "For I reckon that the sufferings of this present time are not worthy to be compared with the glory which shall be revealed in us."

IN CLOSING

We know we have entered the last of the last days when political, religious, and cultural happenings take upon the character and fulfillment of the final prophetic events. With the rise to world dominance of Great Britain, the United States, and Russia, we know we are approaching earth's final years.

With the increasing influence of Islam, we know the leopard empire is positioning itself to establish the environment for the Antichrist's arrival. The leopard, increasing in power, signals that the ten-region political/economic realignment will soon be set in place, and then the Antichrist will make his appearance.

Our world leaders are looking forward to this time as they openly move their nations toward this global economic and political realignment. This realignment is summed up in the term, *New World Order.* This term is used consistently by

Timeline 2: Toward the Final Years

world leaders to refer to the development of a new world structure that unites all the economies and nations of the world into ten economic/political regions. Pay close attention to how world leaders use variations of this term. This phrase will inform us to how close we are to its fulfillment.

TIMELINE 2: DANIEL 7

1707 AD	Great Britain	Lion	7:4
1776 AD	United States	Eagle Wings	7:4
1922 AD	Russia	Bear	7:5
CURRENT	Islam	Leopard	7:6
20?? AD	New World Order	4th Beast	7:7
20?? AD	The Antichrist	Little horn	7:8
20?? AD	Christ as God appears for judgment		7:9-14

ARE WE THERE YET?

CHAPTER 4

Timelines 3 & 4
The Countdown Begins
Daniel 9; Matthew 24

DANIEL'S TIMELINES IN DANIEL 2 AND 7 REVEALED THE EMPIRES THAT LEAD THE WORLD INTO EARTH'S FINAL DAYS. IN DANIEL 9, A TIMELINE IS RECORDED THAT connects the timelines of Daniel 2 and Daniel 7, transitioning the world through the last days to the last of the last days and earth's final seven years.

At the time Daniel 9 was written, the Israelites were in captivity. Daniel understood from the prophet Jeremiah that they were to be in Babylon for seventy years.[109] Daniel also knew the seventy-years were at its end. Through prayer and searching the Scripture, he wanted to know if their freedom was imminent. Part of what Daniel read was most likely Jeremiah 25:9-11 (underline added):

> "Behold, I will send and take all the families of the north, says the Lord, and Nebuchadrezzar the king of Babylon,

---

109 Daniel 9:2

> my servant, and will bring them against this land, and against the inhabitants thereof, and against all these nations round about, and will utterly destroy them, and make them an astonishment, and an hissing, and perpetual desolations. Moreover I will take from them the voice of mirth, and the voice of gladness, the voice of the bridegroom, and the voice of the bride, the sound of the millstones, and the light of the candle. And this whole land shall be desolation, and astonishment; <u>and these nations shall serve the king of Babylon seventy years."</u>

Though Daniel understood the captivity would last seventy years, and was now at its end, there was much he did not understand. What he heard from the angel Gabriel was more than he bargained for, as we will now find out.

DAYS EQUALS YEARS

Imagine asking someone about seventy *years*, as recorded in the above passage in Jeremiah, and receiving an answer about seventy *weeks*. Certainly, you and I may be a little confused. Yet this is the answer the angel Gabriel gave to Daniel—and Daniel knew exactly what he meant. Daniel understood that one week was equal to seven years, with each day of the week being one year.[110]

This concept was very much part of Jewish thought and is seen when Jacob agreed to work for his future father-in-law Laban for one week in order to marry his daughter Rachel.[111] It was understood by both men that the "one week" meant seven years with one day being equivalent to

---
110 Daniel 9:20-24
111 Genesis 29:15-18

Timelines 3 & 4: The Countdown Begins

one year. Also, when God breached[112] His promise to bring Israel into the Promise Land because of their sin, they were told they would be punished for forty days, with each day equivalent to one year.[113]

Daniel's accounting of time would have seen one day as one year. Therefore, the seventy years would have equaled seven days multiplied by seventy weeks to equal four hundred ninety years of troubles that the Israelites would yet experience—not just their present seventy years of captivity. The captivity in Babylon was only the beginning of God's wrath toward Israel. Though the Israelites were released from their seventy years of captivity in Babylon, they still were not released from God's anger due to their sin.

The angel further divided the seventy weeks into seven weeks, sixty-two weeks, and one week. The first seven weeks multiplied by seven days equals forty-nine years and is referenced in Daniel 9:25:

> "Know therefore and understand, that from the going forth of the commandment to restore and to build Jerusalem unto the Messiah the Prince shall be seven weeks, and threescore and two weeks: the street shall be built again, and the wall, even in troublous times."

This commandment refers to the decree issued by Arterxerxes in 445 BC, as recorded in Nehemiah 2:1-8, to the

---

[112] Numbers 14:34
[113] Numbers 14:34

ARE WE THERE YET?

completion of the rebuilding of Jerusalem forty-nine years later.[114]

The sixty-two weeks multiplied by seven days equals four hundred thirty-four years and refers to the time that Jerusalem was rebuilt up to the time that Christ was crucified.[115]

After Christ's death and resurrection, Jerusalem and the temple were once again destroyed by the Romans and the people they recruited to fight with them in 70 AD.[116]

Jerusalem and the temple would remain desolate and the Jews scattered until 1948 when Israel became a nation again, the Jews began returning to Israel, and the desert land began to bloom with fruits and vegetables. I like Mark Twain's observation of Israel when he visited in 1867. This well describes Israel's barren condition prior to 1948:

> "We traversed some miles of desolate country whose soil is rich enough, but is given over wholly to weeds – a silent, mournful expanse....The further we went the hotter the sun got, and the more rocky and bare, repulsive and dreary the landscape became. There could not have been more fragments of stone strewn broadcast over this part of the world, if every ten square feet of the land had been occupied by a separate and distinct stonecutter's establishment for an age. There was hardly a tree or a shrub anywhere. Even the olive

---

[114] Daniel 9:25-26 Concerning the decree, there are questions concerning which decree should be used as there were three that are identified as possible. The other two was the decree issued by King Cyrus in 537 BC (Isaiah 44:28, 45:1) and the decree issued by Darius I in 520 BC (Ezra 6:1-12). The important thing in our context is that there was an actual historical decree and that the events outlined in Daniel actually took place as recorded.
[115] Daniel 9:25
[116] Daniel 9:26

Timelines 3 & 4: The Countdown Begins

and the cactus, those fast friends of a worthless soil, had almost deserted the country. No landscape exists that is more tiresome to the eye than that which bounds the approaches to Jerusalem. The only difference between the roads and the surrounding country, perhaps, is that there are rather more rocks in the roads than in the surrounding country."[117]

After over twenty-five hundred years of being desolate, a recent author made this observation of Israel's present condition after reforming as a nation:

"In so many ways, Biblical prophecies are being fulfilled before our very eyes since Israel has become a nation once again. It wasn't that long ago that this land truly was desolate and bereft of life. And now? Every year, Israel not only grows enough for national consumption, we export annually more than 2 billion dollars worth of produce to the markets of the world. And as if that weren't enough, Israel also exports millions of flowers! On Valentine's Day, for example, Israel exported 60 million flowers to the markets of Europe—the Netherlands, Germany, Switzerland, Italy and England! We are able to grow flowers year-round, which helps fill international demand for flowers in all seasons.

Not only that, everything grows beautifully. To quote Israel 21c org/environment, 'Every year Israel exports more than $2 billion worth of produce—tomatoes are its fourth-largest commodity—and is among the world's top developers of better-tasting, better-looking, disease-resistant and more nutritious varieties.'" [118]

---

[117] Mark Twain, Innocent's Abroad (Hartford, CN: American Publishing 1869) Chapter 47.
[118] Esther Korson, The Land of Israel: From Desolation to Abundance (thejerusalemgiftshop.com: May 17, 2014).

ARE WE THERE YET?

Together, the seven weeks and sixty-two weeks equals sixty-nine of the seventy weeks revealed to Daniel. Daniel records the last week (7 years) as the time when the Antichrist arrives, confirms a seven-year treaty with Israel, breaks the treaty, and ushers in the great tribulation.[119]

Since we have a period of time much longer than 490 years (70 weeks) between the 69th and 70th week, we have what is traditionally called a pause, located between the death of Jesus and the arrival of the Antichrist and is what we call the last days, the times of the gentiles, and the days of harvest.[120]

Here's the timeline of Daniel's 70 weeks:

TIMELINE 3: DANIEL 9

445 BC	Decree to rebuild temple	9:25
396 BC	Completion of Jerusalem to death of Christ	9:25, 26
34 AD	Death of Christ to last days/pause	9:26
20?? AD	Age of the Antichrist, great tribulation	9:27

THE COUNTDOWN

What takes place between the 69th and 70th weeks is a transition period that leads to the age of the Antichrist. The events of this period will increase and become more frequent until we reach the arrival of the Antichrist. These events are

---

[119] Daniel 9:27
[120] Daniel 9:26-27

Timelines 3 & 4: The Countdown Begins

outlined in Matthew 24 and is that period known as the last days and the Christian era.

The arrival of Jesus and the Christian era suspends the normal accounting of years revealed to Daniel. The reason for this pause is to call out from the world all who will respond to repent of their sin and look forward to the eternal life to come. During this time, God not only gives the opportunity of an eternal inheritance to Abraham's physical descendants, but to any individual of any nation or people.

Some are puzzled by the length of Jesus' promise that He would come back soon. The Apostle Peter was contemporary with Jesus. After Jesus' death, and many years later, people questioned what Christ had said about coming back soon. In response, Peter replied in 2 Peter 3:8-9:

> "But, beloved, be not ignorant of this one thing, that one day is with the Lord as a thousand years, and a thousand years as one day. The Lord is not slack concerning his promise, as some men count slackness; but is longsuffering to us-ward, not willing that any should perish, but that all should come to repentance."

The Apostle reminds us that God does not count time in the same way that we do and is patient, not wanting anyone to perish. Therefore, He will not fulfill His promise to Abraham until the last person who will receive His inheritance has been conceived and given this opportunity. This is why this pause has lasted for over two thousand years, but those days are ending quickly.

According to Daniel 2, 7, and Matthew 24, the 70th week (last seven years) is close at hand. Jesus appeared on earth to usher in the last days, to inform us of what was coming, and to instruct us on how to get ready for the final week. He came to call us to prepare for earth's final years when he taught:

> "The time is fulfilled, and the kingdom of God is at hand: repent ye, and believe the gospel."[121]

JESUS, THE MILE MARKER

It was Jesus' arrival that marked the beginning to the last days and started the end time's countdown in Matthew 24. This is confirmed by each of the writers of the New Testament.

In Hebrews 9:26, the writer witnessed, "Now once in the end of the world has he [Jesus] appeared to put away sin by the sacrifice of himself." He also writes in Hebrews 1:1-2, "God, who at sundry times and in various manners spoke in time past unto the fathers by the prophets, has in these last days spoken unto us by his Son, whom he has appointed heir of all things, by whom also he made the worlds." These verses reveal the advent of Jesus was also the advent of the last days.

The Apostle Peter confirmed that Jesus ushered in the last days for our benefit: "Who verily was foreordained before the foundation of the world, but was manifest in these last times for you."[122] He also wrote that the last of the last days were close at hand: "But the end of all things is at hand:

---

121 Mark 1:15
122 1 Peter 1:20

Timelines 3 & 4: The Countdown Begins

be ye therefore sober, and watch unto prayer."[123] The Apostle John wrote that the many antichrists in his day was evidence that the last days had come: "It is the last time: and as ye have heard that antichrist shall come, even now are there many antichrists; whereby we know that it is the last time."[124] The Apostle James wrote concerning Christ's second coming that "the coming of the Lord draws near" and that "the judge stands before the door."[125] And Jude spoke of the sinful spirit of his day as taking place "in the last time," the time in which he lived.[126]

Jesus also was clear that He ushered in the last days when He began His public ministry proclaiming, "The time is fulfilled, and the kingdom of God is at hand: repent ye, and believe the gospel."[127] When Jesus taught that "the time is fulfilled," He refers to the fact that everything that needed to be in place before the end of the world began, had taken place. This would also have meant that the empires of Babylon, Medes-Persia, and Greece would have risen and fallen, and that Rome, even then at the height of its power, would soon fall.

Jesus was clear that the last days had now begun, God's kingdom is ready to be revealed, and it is time to prepare to enter His kingdom through repentance and belief in the message He preached. The days since Jesus appeared have been the days for gathering and harvesting God's people, so

---

123 1 Peter 4:7
124 1 John 2:18
125 James 5:8, 9
126 Jude 18-20
127 Mark 1:15

they will be prepared for the coming end of all things. Jesus spoke to His disciples that the harvest was now ready to be brought in:

> "Say not ye, There are yet four months, and then cometh harvest? Behold, I say unto you, Lift up your eyes, and look on the fields; for they are white already to harvest."128

Also, the last command given by Jesus to His disciples in Mark 15:15-16 was to continue this harvesting:

> "And he said unto them, Go ye into all the world, and preach the gospel to every creature. He that believes and is baptized shall be saved; but he that believes not shall be damned."

The above Scriptures reveal we have lived in the last days for over 2000 years, and the event ushering in these days was the appearing of Jesus upon the earth. The arrival of Jesus is the mile marker informing us the last days have arrived and the countdown has begun. Jesus' ministry was earmarked with this awareness and our need to prepare for its end and the eternity to come. Jesus spoke clearly in His Matthew 24 teaching about earth's final days and what to expect from that point on.

COUNTING DOWN

The events and character of this countdown are revealed through three questions asked by the disciples

---

128 John 4:35 See also Matthew 9:37-38; Revelation 14:15

when Jesus answered them informing them about the last days and what to expect in Matthew 24:3: When shall these things be? What shall be the sign of your coming? What shall be the sign of the end of the world?

The statistics of the increase of the events in Matthew 24 are so easily accessible that I will only speak of them briefly in order to focus on the chronology of events. And if, like me, you are a fifties child or older, you have much of this knowledge firsthand having lived through the exponential increases.

THE FIRST QUESTION

The disciples first question is, "When shall these things be?," was a general question. Jesus responded in kind with an overview of the last days in Matthew 24:4-28. This overview records the events leading to the arrival of the Antichrist. What Jesus taught about these times is not a pretty picture. Deception, troubles, natural disasters, disease, and great persecution are the norm. These events are to unfold and increase until the world is filled with great distress, a time the Apostle Paul calls "perilous."[129]

Jesus taught that many disciples would be deceived by those claiming to be Him[130] and there would be wars and rumors of wars.[131] He told them to "be not troubled" by these events, because "all these things must come to pass." In other words, these were just everyday events that would

---

129 2 Timothy 3:1
130 Matthew 24:4,5
131 Ibid

take place throughout all generations and were not signs the end of the world was near—only that it had begun. These events characterize the pause, the last days, from its beginning to its end when the Antichrist arrives.

The events telling us we have entered the last of the last days, and puts in place the last events necessary for the Antichrist to arise, are those recorded in Matthew 24:7, 8:

> "For nation [ethnos] shall rise against nation [ethnos], and kingdom against kingdom: and there shall be famines, and pestilences, and earthquakes, in various places. All these are the beginning of sorrows."

The distinction between "ethnos" and kingdom is that "ethnos" is the Greek word referring to ethnic and racial groups as well as smaller nations, while kingdom refers to the conflicts of empires such as WWI, WWII, and now with Islam.

All these events are called "the beginning of sorrows." Other translations interpret this as "the beginning of birth pains." Both refer to the idea that these events would increase in frequency and intensity until reaching the point when the intensity and frequency will be almost unbearable. These events are so widespread and frequent today that they have become every day events, yet have not reached the intensity that makes them almost unbearable.

Also during the "beginning of sorrows," the global persecution of Christians and Jews will increase until the sorrows become the great sorrows of the great tribulation. During this time Christians will have much pressure put upon them. Many will be thrown into prison. Many will be

Timelines 3 & 4: The Countdown Begins

killed. God's people will be greatly hated because of their trust in Jesus. Many Christians will not like what they see happening to fellow Christians. In order to preserve their own lives, many claiming the name of Christ will betray and hate their fellow Christians.[132] This all sounds as if being a Christian or Jew will become illegal and those coming against fellow Christians will think they are doing service to God.[133] As we observed in chapter one, persecution is greatly increasing and moving toward the horrific holocaust of Jews and Christians and anyone opposed to the Antichrist's agenda.

The beginning of sorrows also will see many deceived by "false prophets" who add to, take away from, and pervert Scripture to fulfill their own desires.[134] Because of all the deception and persecution, many Christians will lose their love and compassion.[135] The key to surviving these very difficult times, with our faith still with us, is simply to *endure*.[136]

These will not be times we are taken out of, but times we must experience and endure. To endure is to hold on until what we are going through is over or we are dead. In the midst of all the suffering, the good news of Jesus Christ will have been heard in all nations.[137] Once everyone has had the opportunity of hearing the good news, the final events of the

---

[132] Matthew 24:10
[133] John 16:2
[134] Matthew 24:11
[135] Matthew 24:12
[136] Matthew 24:13
[137] Matthew 24:14

end of our present age will appear. The Gospel taken to all nations has taken place. The time is short.

These final events of the last days outlines earth's final seven years, the fulfillment of the book of Revelation, and the great tribulation of God's people. These are the times the Apostle Paul calls "perilous," dangerous times.[138] Matthew 24:15, 21 records when this great tribulation will appear:

> "When ye therefore shall see the abomination of desolation, spoken of by Daniel the prophet, stand in the holy place, (whoso reads, let him understand). For then shall be great tribulation, such as was not since the beginning of the world to this time, no, nor ever shall be."

The abomination of desolation is the sign revealing that all hell will be unleashed upon the Jews, Christians, and all who oppose the Antichrist and his new world order. This abomination is the Antichrist. Daniel 12:11 indicates this abomination appears after the temple is rebuilt. The Antichrist cannot be in the temple if the temple is not there. So horrible will be this future persecution that no other historical persecution past or present can compare to it.[139] This holocaust will be so horrible that if God did not shorten how long it would last, not even the strongest of His people would be saved.[140]

To get through these terrible days, we will need to hold on to the words of Jesus here in Matthew 24. He has given His

---

[138] 2 Timothy 3:1
[139] Matthew 24:21
[140] Matthew 24:22

Timelines 3 & 4: The Countdown Begins

warnings so we may find assurance in His Word and courage to endure.[141] God's Word is true. God's Word is certain. God's Word reveals greater things for those who hold on just a little while longer—don't let go!

THE SECOND QUESTION

All of the events in the first question leads us through the last days and signals how close we are to Christ's coming. What is revealed is that we are now living at the end of that time known as the "beginning of sorrows" and will soon experience the arrival of the Antichrist and the great tribulation. This then leads to this second question: "What shall be the sign of your coming?"

In answer, Jesus reveals a specific sign to let us know He will appear within any moment. Before this sign is revealed, the sun and moon will lose their light, the stars will fall from the sky, and all of the heavens will be shaken; this all happens *immediately after the great tribulation*.[142] It is after this celestial show that the *sign of the son of man* will appear.[143] By emphasizing to His disciples that they will be able to see the "sign of the son of man," indicates the disciples were aware of the sign and what it was. There are only two signs recorded in the Bible relating to Jesus. The first is found in Isaiah 7:14:

---

141 Matthew 24:25-28
142 Matthew 24:29
143 Matthew 24:30

ARE WE THERE YET?

> "Therefore the Lord himself shall give you a sign; Behold, a virgin shall conceive, and bear a son, and shall call his name Immanuel."

This cannot be the sign Jesus spoke of since it was not seen in the sky and had been fulfilled when Christ was born. The second sign is recorded in Matthew 2:2 when the wise men from the east asked:

> "Where is he that is born King of the Jews? for we have seen his star in the east, and are come to worship him."

Note that the wise men called this star *"his star."* They followed this specific star to the city where Jesus was born.[144] This could be the sign Jesus refers to. It meets all the criteria: it was seen from the sky and is connected with Jesus as the "son of man."

Daniel the prophet also gives credence to a star or planet from heaven being the sign of the Son of man when he writes of a future "stone not made with hands" that will come out of heaven to destroy the Antichrist's kingdom.[145] This stone most likely refers to a star/planet representing Christ, the one who will destroy the Devil's earthly body/empires.[146]

Another consideration is that when the powers of the heavens are shaken, the sun and moon no longer gives light, and the stars fall from heaven, this may be the sign preceding Christ's coming. All three gospels speak of the events in the

---

[144] Matthew 2:9-10
[145] Daniel 2:34-35, 45
[146] For a study on a star/planet being the sign of Christ's coming, check out, Planet X:The Sign of the Son of Man by Douglas A. Elwell.

Timelines 3 & 4: The Countdown Begins

sky preceding Christ's appearance in the clouds.[147] There is a question whether this is the sign because Matthew 24:29, 30 is the only one who records that the "sign of the Son of man" will take place after the events in the sky occur.

I lean toward the position that the events in the sky and the appearing of Christ take place at the same time, with Christ's appearing on a planet/star causing the apocalyptic motion in the heavens as He enters earth's galaxy.

THE THIRD QUESTION

Jesus answers the disciples third question, "What shall be the sign of the world's end?," by referring to the gathering of His people by the angels. This is the sign that lets us know the world's last hour has come. Matthew 24:31, 32 is clear that, after Jesus appears, He sends His angels to the earth to gather His people to where He is.

> "And he shall send his angels with a great sound of a trumpet, and they shall gather together his elect from the four winds, from one end of heaven to the other. 32 Now learn a parable of the fig tree; When his branch is yet tender, and putteth forth leaves, ye know that summer is nigh:"

This is the rapture. It takes place after the great tribulation. As we follow Jesus' ordering of events, there is no question when the rapture takes place.

Additional details of what this gathering by the angels will look like are described in Matthew 24:37-44:

---

[147] Matthew 24:29-30; Mark 13:25-26; Luke 21:26-27

ARE WE THERE YET?

> "But as the days of Noah were, so shall also the coming of the Son of man be. For as in the days that were before the flood they were eating and drinking, marrying and giving in marriage, until the day that Noah entered into the ark, And knew not until the flood came, and took them all away; so shall also the coming of the Son of man be.
>
> Then shall two be in the field; the one shall be taken, and the other left. Two women shall be grinding at the mill; the one shall be taken, and the other left. Watch therefore: for ye know not what hour your Lord does come. But know this, that if the goodman of the house had known in what watch the thief would come, he would have watched, and would not have suffered his house to be broken up. Therefore be ye also ready: for in such an hour as ye think not the Son of man cometh."

Notice that Jesus links His coming and the rapture together when He encouraged, after teaching about the rapture, "Therefore be ye also ready: for in such an hour as ye think not the Son of man comes."

It is this rapture that answers the disciple's third question and is the sign that the world has less than sixty minutes left—literally a sixty-second minute,[148] and not the popular view of seven years.[149]

Matthew 24 is clear on when the rapture takes place: the world will grow worse, persecution will increase, the Antichrist will appear, the great tribulation will come, the heavens will be shaken, Jesus will appear, and then the rapture will occur. We do not need to move from the clear

---

[148] Revelation 14:7, 3:10; Matthew 24:36
[149] For more information on this sixty minutes, see my commentary on the book of Revelation: "Revelation and the Age of the Antichrist."

Timelines 3 & 4: The Countdown Begins

teaching of Scripture to understand when the rapture will happen.

This order of events also is outlined in the book of Daniel and the book of Revelation, as seen in the chart below. When we follow the sequence of events in each chapter, and the natural sequence of verses (1, 2, 3, etc.), the events of the last days fall into the same order in each of these books. We do not need to reason the ordering into place, or create our own timeline; we only need to read the order as it is given.

COMPARISON OF LAST DAY EVENTS

EVENT	DANIEL	MATT 24	REVELATION
Apostasy	Israel in Apostasy	24:4-5	2&3
Antichrist	7:19,20,23,24	24:15	6:3-9
	8:9,10,23,24		
	9:27		
	11:11-30		
Great	7:21,25	24:9-22	6:3-9
Tribulation	8:11,14,24		
	9:27		
	11:31-36		
	12:1		
Revival	11:32		11:3-10
Christ Returns	7:22,26	24:29,30	11:12-16
			14:15,16
Rapture	12:1	24:31	11:11,12
			14:15,16
Eternity	12:2,3		19:11,12

ARE WE THERE YET?

WE CAN KNOW

When we understand the timelines given to Daniel, Jesus, and the Apostle John, there is no question concerning the ordering of last day events.

Jesus meant for us to be certain about the end times and His return. He did not call us to be philosophers pondering the events and developing elaborate theories and speculation concerning them. He made this clear when He taught, "When <u>you shall see</u> all these things, <u>know that</u> it is near, even at the doors;"[150] He said as well, "<u>Watch therefore</u>: for you know not what hour your Lord does come."[151] We cannot "see," "know," or be on the "watch" for events that cannot be measured with certainty. These events let us know how close we are to the age of the Antichrist and the return of Christ.

Also, after teaching about the events of the last days, Jesus then gave the assurance:

> "So likewise ye, when ye shall see all these things, know that it is near, even at the doors."[152]

Jesus is clear that we can know where we are on the prophetic timeline by observing the specific events He told us about.

Jesus also made the statement concerning these events: "Behold, I have told you before,"[153] indicating that we are without excuse for not knowing the events of the last days

---

[150] Matthew 24:33
[151] Matthew 24:42
[152] Matthew 24:33
[153] Matthew 24:25

when they are upon us. Jesus taught about the events of the last days to give certainty of the prophetic times we are living in.

Since Jesus' appearance, the events in Matthew 24 would increase until their frequency and intensity become so great that not even Christians would be saved if Christ did not intervene. This is why each generation speaks of how their generation is worse than the one before them. Each successive generation is worse than the previous one and will continue to grow worse until the Antichrist arrives, releasing the great tribulation on earth.[154] The last days leading to the return of Christ is nothing more than an increase in quantity, intensity, and frequency of the world situation causing tremendous pressure to survive, especially as a Christian or Jew. Eventually we will enter into that time the Apostle Paul calls *perilous times*—the age of the Antichrist.

IN CLOSING

Daniel's outline of the 70 weeks reveals a pause between the 69th and 70th week. This pause is what we call the last days and is outlined in Jesus teaching in Matthew 24.

When Jesus appeared, this began the countdown to the end of our present age. He taught that the events taking place during this time would lead to the last of the last days and the arrival of the Antichrist. He also outlined our responsibility

---

[154] When comparing generations, many make the mistake and compare decades. When a generation of seventy years is compared, vast differences from one generation to the next are seen; for example, 1830 with 1900; 1900 with 1970; or 1970 with the present year.

ARE WE THERE YET?

to help bring in the harvest before these days arrive and cautioned us to make sure that we are not Christian only in appearance, but to live with the power of the Holy Spirit alive and active within us.

The last days timeline outlined in Matthew 24 lets us know that we are now in that period called "the beginning of sorrows." This will lead to the arrival of the Antichrist and the great tribulation. With Christian persecution on the rise globally, we can be certain we are nearing the end of the "beginning of sorrows."

The time is short. Let us proclaim the coming good news.

Timeline 4 is on the next page.

Timelines 3 & 4: The Countdown Begins

TIMELINE 4: MATTHEW 24

34 AD	Everyday Events False Christ's Wars Rumors of Wars	24:4-6
1914 AD[155]	Beginning of Sorrows Nation against Nation Kingdom against Kingdom Famines Diseases Earthquakes	24:7, 8
20?? AD	Great Tribulation Global Persecution Hyperinflation Violence	24:9-28
20?? AD	Sign of Christ's Coming	24:29-35
20?? AD	Rapture	24:36-41

---

[155] 1914, the beginning of WWI, is the date the first truly global war involving the majority of nations aligning with one side or the other took place. Since kingdom against kingdom is a sign that we have entered the last of the last days and the beginning of sorrows, the date for WWI is used.

ARE WE THERE YET?

CHAPTER 5

Timeline 5
Age of the Antichrist
Revelation 1-22

IN THE PREVIOUS CHAPTERS, WE SAW HOW DANIEL 2, 7, 9, AND MATTHEW 24 ALL BROUGHT US TO THE AGE OF THE ANTICHRIST. IN THIS CHAPTER, WE LOOK AT THE AGE OF the Antichrist outlined in the book of Revelation.

The Revelation given to the Apostle John is the timeline of earth's final seven years written in chronological order. This is the seventieth week of Daniel's 70 weeks, and the time when the new world order has been established and the Antichrist is in power. On the prophetic timeline, the age of the Antichrist is placed after the ten nation new world order is in place.

This chapter summarizes the book of Revelation to show the timeline it presents. For a more detailed commentary on the book of Revelation, check out my book, *Revelation and the Age of the Antichrist*.

ARE WE THERE YET?

THE GREAT APOSTASY

Earth's last seven years begins with a great apostasy, an apostasy so great that the majority claiming the name of Christ will not know Him. In harmony with the Apostle Paul, the book of Revelation places the great apostasy before the revealing of the Antichrist. It is this apostasy that lays out the welcome mat for the Antichrist. The Apostle writes in 2 Thessalonians 2:3:

> "Let no man deceive you by any means: for that day shall not come, except there come a falling away first, and that man of sin be revealed, the son of perdition."

In the book of Revelation, the apostasy is also outlined in chapters 2 and 3 prior to the revealing of the Antichrist in chapter 6. The character of this apostasy is described through the seven churches. In each of these, the characteristic of the church throughout history is outlined. Even though the positive characteristics are desired by all Christians, Christ encourages five of the seven to repent because they conformed, added to their Christianity, or embraced teachings contrary to Christianity. They had what the Apostle Paul called in 2 Timothy 3:5 an "image" of being a Christian without the Holy Spirit to be Christian:

> "This know also, that in the last days perilous times shall come...Having a form of godliness, but denying the power thereof: from such turn away."

What makes us Christian is not our good, Christian works—it is the Holy Spirit alive and active within us. The

Timeline 5: Age of the Antichrist

Apostle Paul made this clear when he wrote, "Now if any man have not the Spirit of Christ, he is none of his."[156]

Put another way, you may be a good Methodist without the Holy Spirit, but you can never be a Christian without the Holy Spirit. This is not picking on the Methodist. You can belong to any denomination and be a good "church" person without ever being a Christian. Yes, even a strong, firm, staunch Baptist may be just that...but never be Christian.

The five apostate churches reveal that departure from Christ does not always mean a departure from the doctrines and works and disciplines of Christ, but the adding to and embracing of that which is not of God. Many who claim to be Christian and gay, Christian and living with someone without marriage, Christian and Wicca, Christian and Jewish, or Christian and...fill in the blank...may truly be Christian in doctrine and works, but not Christian in relationship with God and spirit. The end result is not being a Christian at all.

The apostasy of the church has increased greatly since the church was born. In these days before the Antichrist, the apostasy is so great that the majority claiming the name of Christ do not know Him, having only the image of being a Christian without the power to be Christian. I make this statement based on Scripture, not on observation. Observation would not be able to discern those who were Christian in every way, but without the Holy Spirit....which makes them not a Christian at all. It is this apostasy which is the welcome mat inviting the Antichrist and his hoard of fallen angels to appear on the earth. If we acknowledge that

---

[156] Romans 8:9

ARE WE THERE YET?

we are living at the time when we expect the Antichrist to appear, and Christ to return, then we must also acknowledge that the majority claiming the name of Christ do not know Him.

The wide difference between the five apostate and the two faithful churches are massive. The five apostate churches did not have the same experience as the two faithful churches at Smyrna and Philadelphia. The faithful's experience was filled with:

- Christian works (Rev. 2:9; 3:8)
- Tribulation (Rev. 2:9)
- Poverty (Rev. 2:9)
- Blasphemed by others (Rev 2:9)
- Thrown into prison (Rev. 2:10)
- Death (Rev. 2:10)
- Faithful to God's Word (Rev. 3:8; 10)
- Not denying Christ in tribulation (Rev. 3:8)

When the churches in the United States are compared with the faithful churches in the Revelation, we must acknowledge that with all of its wealth, pomp, and good standing in the community, the church has traveled a long distance from the path of truly being Christian. This apostasy began when the church began. As it continues to increase, the church's power decreases. When the power decreases, entertainment, good works, and the holding onto doctrines increase. It is this lack of the Holy Spirit that welcomes the Antichrist with open arms.

Timeline 5: Age of the Antichrist

When I speak of this apostasy to others, it is rare that someone will consider that maybe they or their denomination are in apostasy. Many will take offense at even the suggestion and become highly defensive. My encouragement to all is to not brush aside the great possibility that you are one of the deceived. Earnestly consider your Christianity in light of the faithful and apostate churches here in Revelation 2 and 3. Be honest. Be objective. Our times demand it. Your eternal destiny depends upon it.

3 ½ YEARS OF 7 SEALS
THE GREAT TRIBULATION
WRATH OF ANTICHRIST

After the apostasy welcomes the Antichrist, he will then be released on the earth through the events taking place in heaven in Revelation 4 and 5.

In chapter 4 of Revelation, God is shown to be worthy to sit upon His throne and to give the seven sealed book to Christ to release earth's final seven years. In chapter 5, Christ is found worthy to receive the seven sealed book from God. After receiving the book, He opens its seals to release the Antichrist and his horrors upon the earth.

During the Antichrist's rule, there will be a global holocaust of Jews, Christians, and anyone opposed to him.[157] Violence will be uncontrolled.[158] Hyperinflation will take place on a global level, causing a great divide between the

---

157 Revelation 12:17
158 Revelation 6:4

rich and poor.[159] Martyrdom and death will be so pervasive that one fourth of the people on earth will die.[160] The majority of the one fourth killed are revealed in 6:9-11 to be God's people. The majority belonging to God will be killed at this time. There will be no rapture before this great tribulation. As we move toward the great tribulation, these events will continue to increase until the Antichrist arrives to usher us into very dangerous and perilous times.

3 ½ YEARS OF 7 TRUMPETS
THE GREAT REVIVAL
WRATH OF CHRIST

After the Antichrist's three and one half years of terror, God sends a great earthquake upon the earth as if to say, "Antichrist, that's enough!" [161]

In heaven, preparations are made to release the wrath of Christ, which is the blowing of the seven trumpets. A distinction is made here between the wrath released by the Antichrist, the wrath of Christ, and the wrath of God. In this preparation, 144,000 birth-born Israelites are sealed with God's protective seal.[162]

After the preparations, the wrath of Christ is poured out in the form of the trumpet judgments.[163] During this time, the Jewish and Christian remnants are empowered through the Holy Spirit to execute judgment in Christ's name in the

---

159 Revelation 6:5,6
160 Revelation 6:5-11
161 Revelation 6:12
162 Revelation 7:4-8
163 Revelation 8-11

Timeline 5: Age of the Antichrist

manner of Elijah and Moses.[164] These remnants are known as the two witnesses of Revelation 11.[165] For three and one half years these witnesses prophecy during the three and one half years of the great tribulation brought by the Antichrist. This is also known as the "great revival" which many look forward to, but never knows exactly when it will take place. Through the great tribulation fire, the Holy Spirit is released and God's people are empowered to do exploits reminiscent of Elijah and Moses.

So much has happened with the opening of the seals and the blowing of the trumpets that Revelation 12 and 13 give more details concerning the personalities involved and the great battle of the ages that is revealed up to this point.

This present battle had its beginnings with Israel, represented here as a "woman clothed with the sun," who gives birth to the Christ. The Devil is against Christ's birth, knowing that His birth would mean his total separation from God and all that he has known. In his opposition the Devil incites a rebellion in heaven among the angels, causing one third of the angels to join him on earth to stop Christ's birth. The Devil does not succeed. Christ grows, develops as a man, and completes the work God sent Him to do. After completing God's work, the Devil crucifies Christ. He dies, but death does not keep Him. He defeats death and ascends to heaven to sit on the throne that is at the right hand of God's throne.

---

[164] Revelation 11:6
[165] See my book, "Revelation and the Age of the Antichrist" for more information about Israel and the Church being the two witnesses.

ARE WE THERE YET?

When Israel became a nation again, another battle took place in heaven between Michael and his angels and the Devil and his angels. The Devil loses the battle and is cast out with his angels *into* the physical earth. Now inside the earth, he and his angels influence the world to receive the Antichrist through politics, religion, education, culture, and the various systems of the nations.

To help him in this task, the two horns of the false prophet (Catholicism and Islam) influence the beliefs and hearts of the people toward the Antichrist, eventually culminating as the final false prophet of Catholicism, the Pope, and the final messiah of the Muslims, the Mahdi. These false prophets encourage all to receive the new world order and the economic mark of the Antichrist's system. Those that don't will not be able to buy or sell, pay rent, pay medical expenses, pay utilities, etc.. More details of these false prophets are in my book, *Revelation and the Age of the Antichrist*.

1 HOUR OF 7 VIALS
THE GREAT WRATH
WRATH OF GOD

Revelation 14-19 gives insight into God's hour of wrath. Before God's hour of wrath is poured out on the earth with the seven vials, preparations are made in heaven to prepare for the return of Christ to Mt. Zion. He will return with the martyred 144,000 Israelites to complete the judgment of the earth and its Babylonian spirit.

Timeline 5: Age of the Antichrist

After His return, God's people are raptured out and those left upon the earth suffer God's hour of wrath through the pouring out of the seven vial judgments.[166] This is that judgment known as the "day and hour" of God's wrath. This is a specific day and a specific hour which takes place in a specific month and year. It is not a season or period of time as some have suggested.

Everyone now left on the earth will experience God's wrath, for none are His people. Everything necessary to sustain life will disappear. All water will become undrinkable, the sun will stop giving light, and every city, island, and mountain will disappear[167] –all within one hour. Sounds like a lot takes place within a short sixty minutes: the return of Christ, the rapture, the pouring out of the seven vials; but we must keep in mind that God created out of nothing the entire universe and all things within it, visible and invisible, in six days. His return, the rapture of His people, and the pouring out of His wrath is nothing in comparison.

In Revelation 17 and 18 we are given understanding to why the earth will be judged, revealing a world system in opposition to God that embraces all manner of sin and unrighteousness. God's judgment does not go well with the Devil or the people on earth as they continue to blaspheme Him, blaming Him for what is taking place.

In response to the coming of Christ, one more effort is made to destroy Christ as four angels gather the militaries of

---

166 Revelation 14-15
167 Revelation 16

the earth to a place called Armageddon to fight against Him. Christ appears riding on a white horse. His great angelic army, also on white horses, is with Him. The people who are left on the earth do not belong to God, and are now killed. Their bodies provide the great feast for what is called the *marriage supper of the lamb*. The marriage supper takes place to clean up the dead bodies that are now everywhere.[168]

1,000 YEARS OF PEACE ON EARTH
REVELATION 20:4-15

After the battle at Armageddon, those martyred by the Antichrist have the privilege to rule with Christ for one thousand years. After the one thousand years, the Devil is released from his prison to deceive many nations to fight one last battle against God's people and God. This is the battle with Gog and Magog.[169] The battle is short as God swiftly defeats the Devil and throws him into the lake of fire. God's great white throne appears, and the present heaven and earth are completely melted and dissolved. The judgment of all—saint and sinner—will now take place at the great white throne judgment.[170] All now enter their final reward or judgment in either eternal life or an eternal lake of fire.

---

168 Revelation 19:1-9; 17-18
169 Revelation 20:8
170 Revelation 20:3-15

Timeline 5: Age of the Antichrist

ENTRANCE INTO ETERNITY
REVELATION 21-22

After all the horrors, we are given a glimpse into our eternal reward in the new heaven and new earth in Revelation 21 and 22. It is as we focus on the inheritance that will be ours that we are able to endure whatever hardships we may have to endure.[171] The book of Revelation is given to the church as a book of hope. While it records the horrors that are coming, it tells us to hold on just a little while longer as we focus on the reward that will be given.

We are given the details of what will take place during earth's last seven years so that when we see the events taking place, we can have full confidence in Christ's word. We can have full assurance that the promise of eternal life and entrance into the new heaven and earth will be given to us after the Antichrist's reign of terror is complete. We need to keep our eyes focused on the rewards that will be ours as we endure the pain and suffering we may soon experience:

> "For I reckon that the sufferings of this present time are not worthy to be compared with the glory which shall be revealed in us."[172]

Timeline 5 is on the next page

---

171 Romans 8:18
172 Romans 8:18

ARE WE THERE YET?

TIMELINE 5: BOOK OF REVELATION

30 AD	to present – Church in Apostasy	2 & 3
20?? AD	The Antichrist arrives	6:1, 2
20?? AD	Great Trib by the Antichrist	6:2-17
20?? AD	Revival of God's people	11:3-13
20?? AD	Christ returns/Rapture	14:14-16
20?? AD	God's day & hour judgment	16:1-18:24
20?? AD	Armageddon	16:16
20?? AD	Marriage supper of the lamb	19:9, 17, 18
20?? AD	Millennium	20:4
30?? AD	Gog and Magog	20:7, 8
30?? AD	Great White Throne Judgment	20:11-15
30?? AD	Eternal Reward & Punishment	21 & 22

CHAPTER 6

The Prophetic Timeline
from the books of Daniel, Matthew, and Revelation

OUR TIMELINE IN DANIEL 2 REVEALS THE NATIONS THAT MAKE UP THE DEVIL'S BODY ON EARTH, STARTING WITH BABYLON AND ENDING WITH THE FINAL EARTHLY EMPIRE of the fourth beast.

Daniel 7's timeline reveals the empires completing the Devil's body and that establishes the Antichrist's kingdom, the new world order of the fourth beast. The timeline in Matthew 24 reveals the events that are now moving us closer to the Antichrist. The last timeline, the book of Revelation, reveals the age of the Antichrist when he is on the scene. Matthew's timeline reveals we are presently living at the end of the beginning of sorrows. We know this for the following reasons:

ARE WE THERE YET?

1. We are living in the time of the divided Roman Empire.
2. The four empires of Daniel 7 are now on the world stage.
3. We have come through the everyday events of Matthew 24.
4. Global Persecution is greatly increasing as we approach the end of the beginning of sorrows.

The prophetic timeline on the next page includes timelines 1-5 in this book. To view a larger color chart of *the prophetic timeline*, visit www.ageofantichrist.com and click on DOWNLOADS.

The Prophetic Timeline

THE PROPHETIC TIMELINE

608 BC Babylon	Head of Gold	Dan. 2:32
538 BC Medes-Persia	Breast & Arms of Silver	Dan. 2:37, 38
445 BC Decree to rebuild temple		Dan. 9:25
396 BC Completion of Jerusalem to death of Christ		Dan. 9:25, 26
333 BC Greece	Belly & Thighs of Brass	Dan. 2:32, 39; 8:21
160 BC Roman Empire	Legs of Iron	Dan. 2:33, 40
30 AD to present	Apostasy	Rev. 2 & 3
34 AD Death of Christ to Last Days		Dan. 9:26
Everyday Events		Mat. 24:4-6
False Christ's		
Wars		
Rumors of Wars		
476 AD	Divided Legs of Iron Roman Empire	Dan. 2:33, 41-43
1707 AD	Great Britain (lion)	Dan. 7:4
1776 AD	United States (eagle wings)	Dan. 7:4
1914 AD Beginning of Sorrows		Mat. 24:7, 8
Nation against Nation		
Kingdom against Kingdom		
Famines		
Diseases		
Earthquakes		
1922 AD	Russia (bear)	Dan. 7:5
Current	Islam (leopard)	Dan. 7:6
20?? AD	4th Beast (New World Order)	Dan. 7:7
20?? AD	The Antichrist (little horn) arrives	Dan. 7:8; 9:27; Rev. 6:1, 2

ARE WE THERE YET?

	Great Tribulation	Mat. 24:9-28
	Global Persecution	Rev. 6:2-4
	Hyperinflation	Rev. 6:5,6
	Violence	Rev. 6:7,8
20?? AD	Revival of God's people	Rev. 11:3-13
20?? AD	Sign of Christ's Coming	Mat. 24:29-35
20?? AD	Christ Returns/Rapture	Dan. 7:9-14; Rev. 14:14-16 Mat. 24:36-41
20?? AD	God's day & hour judgment	Rev. 16:1-18:24
20?? AD	Armageddon	Rev. 16:16
20?? AD	Marriage supper of the lamb	Rev. 19:9, 17,18
20?? AD	God's Kingdom Stone Cut Without Hands	Dan. 2:34, 44,45
20?? AD	Millennium	Rev. 20:4
30?? AD	Gog and Magog	Rev. 20:7, 8
30?? AD	Great White Throne Judgment	Rev. 20:11-15
30?? AD	Eternal Reward and Punishment	Rev. 21 & 22

When the five timelines from Daniel, Matthew, and Revelation are connected with each other according to date order, we have a comprehensive timeline of events leading to the end of all things from around 608 BC to the return of Christ. Following this timeline lets us know the following:

1. The events of the last days
2. The ordering of events
3. Where we are on the prophetic timeline

CHAPTER 7

Our Response
2 Timothy

THE CURRENT GLOBAL PERSECUTION WILL CONTINUE TO INCREASE AND LEAD TO THE GLOBAL HOLOCAUST OF THE ANTICHRIST. PERHAPS EVEN MORE UNSETTLING TO SOME is that there is not much we can do to stop the coming horrors. The encouragement from Scripture is to not take up arms or to physically come against the government or those who oppose us; this type of action belongs to the Antichrist. If we do take this course, the results will turn against us as stated in Revelation 13:10:

> "He that leads into captivity shall go into captivity: he that kills with the sword must be killed with the sword. Here is the patience and the faith of the saints."

God's people have been called to endure and to hold tight to the promises given to us by God. This is why the angel told John, "Here is the patience and the faith of the saints." Much patience will be required in what we will soon be going through. Much faith in the rewards we will receive for enduring must always be before our eyes, knowing as the Apostle Paul in Romans 8:18:

> "For I reckon that the sufferings of this present time are not worthy to be compared with the glory which shall be revealed in us."

WHAT ARE WE TO DO THEN?

Let's look at our great example, Jesus. He is the One who told of these things before they happened so we will be prepared when we experience them.[173] His example was that "His kingdom is not of this world;"[174] therefore, He did not come to defend or give His life for any earthly kingdom. He did not come to possess or claim the world for His Father, but to call others out of the world system. He came not to return evil for evil; therefore, He acted in ways opposite of His oppressors. He did not come to defend His life, but to lay down His life like a sheep led to the slaughter.[175] These are the actions of the One who could have called ten thousand angels to remove Him from the mistreatment He suffered.[176] This is the example we are to follow.

Jesus made the decision to act in ways contrary to this world. He had to make hard choices, even as we must. What helped Him to do what was contrary to the world was His

---

173 John 14:29; Matthew 24:25; Mark 13:23
174 John 18:36
175 Acts 8:32
176 Matthew 26:52

Our Response

faith; He understood the reality of the things that were real, but were not yet in His possession. He was very much aware that His kingdom was not on earth nor had anything to do with this world.[177] He was very much aware that death had been defeated;[178] therefore, His dying was not a defeat, but victory over the world's most feared weapon—death. His death was not a cessation of living, but the beginning of life. It was this awareness that caused the Apostle Paul to write that to leave this life is far better since we will be with Christ.[179]

2 TIMOTHY

Let's look at the encouragements given to Timothy by the Apostle Paul in 2 Timothy. At the time 2 Timothy was written, Paul was in prison and Timothy was experiencing resistance when he confronted false teachers and so called Christians who were participating in behavior that was not of God. All this affected Timothy greatly as tears flowed from his eyes.[180] His shame for the Gospel and even Paul was overtaking him.[181] Fear, weakness, despising of his persecutors, and wrong decisions were increasing within him.[182]

It was in these circumstances that the Apostle Paul puts Timothy in remembrance of his own persecutions and of

---

177 John 18:36
178 1 Corinthians 15:55-57
179 Philippians 1:23,24
180 2 Timothy 1:4
181 2 Timothy 1:8
182 2 Timothy 1:7

ARE WE THERE YET?

what Christ has done for His people.[183] He encouraged Timothy to look at all he had suffered as worth it when compared with the glory that will be given to him. It was in these circumstances that the apostle gave to Timothy his advice on dealing with opposition. What he told him, in a nutshell, was not to treat his adversaries as they treated him or to retreat from their presence. He told Timothy to muster all the gusto he could muster and be more of a Christian and continue to witness with his words and actions whether he was popular or not, whether he suffered or not.[184]

The first thing the Apostle Paul encouraged Timothy to do was to "stir up the gift of God, which is in you." [185] Whether God's Spirit lives and sprouts fruit within you is up to you. God gives the Holy Spirit to us, but He is not going to force His will upon us. It is our responsibility to keep the Spirit alive by using the gifts that are given through the Holy Spirit. This is the encouragement Jesus gave in Matthew 25 after teaching on the last days in Matthew 24.

Matthew 25 is actually part of the Matthew 24 teaching. Jesus' emphasis in teaching about the ten virgins and the ten talents was to encourage his hearers to live in harmony with the Holy Spirit and not rely only upon good works, right doctrine, or Christian discipline. Without the Holy Spirit, we do not belong to Christ (Rom. 8:9).

In the following encouragements the Apostle Paul gave to Timothy, you will note this list is void of any call to retreat or to take up arms or to treat others in the same way we are

---

[183] 2 Timothy 1:8-18
[184] 2 Timothy 4:2
[185] 2 Timothy 1:6

Our Response

treated. It is a definite call to be a witness to the world of the God who created and gave to us His glorious, eternal promises. In this short letter to the discouraged Timothy, I was amazed at how many direct words of encouragement the Apostle Paul gave to him. I will let them speak for themselves here:

1:8 "Be not...ashamed of the testimony of our Lord"

1:8 "Be...partaker of the afflictions of the gospel according to the power of God"

1:13 "Hold fast the form of sound words, which you have heard of me, in faith and love which is in Christ Jesus."

1:14 "That good thing which was committed unto you keep by the Holy Ghost which dwells in us."

2:1 "Be strong in the grace that is in Christ Jesus."

2:2 "The things that you have heard of me among many witnesses, the same commit you to faithful men, who shall be able to teach others also."

2:3 "Endure hardness, as a good soldier of Jesus Christ."

2:15 "Study to show yourself approved unto God, a workman that needs not to be ashamed, rightly dividing the word of truth."

2:16 "Shun profane and vain babblings: for they will increase unto more ungodliness."

2:19 "Let everyone that names the name of Christ depart from iniquity."

2:22 "Flee also youthful lusts: but follow righteousness, faith, charity, peace, with them that call on the Lord out of a pure heart."

2:23 "Foolish and unlearned questions avoid, knowing that they do gender strifes."

2:24-26 "And the servant of the Lord must not strive; but be gentle unto all men, apt to teach, patient, In meekness instructing those that oppose themselves; if God peradventure will give them repentance to the acknowledging of the truth And that they may recover themselves out of the snare of the devil, who are taken captive by him at his will."

3:14 "But continue you in the things which you have learned and have been assured of, knowing of whom you have learned them"

4:2 "Preach the word; be instant in season, out of season; reprove, rebuke, exhort with all long suffering and doctrine."

4:5 "Watch you in all things, endure afflictions, do the work of an evangelist, and make full proof of your ministry."

The Apostle Paul had a lot of encouragement for this suffering saint. Let us also take Paul's encouragements to heart within our own lives. Our twenty-first century is leading to the "perilous" times spoken of by the Apostle. The key to surviving these times is to "stir up" the Holy Spirit within us, ensuring His fire burns through our thoughts, emotions, words, and behavior.

Appendix A
Against All Odds

ISRAEL IS THE FOCUS OF ALL PROPHECY. ALL THE NATIONS LOOKED AT IN THIS BOOK ARE MENTIONED IN SCRIPTURE BECAUSE OF THEIR IMPACT ON ISRAEL. GOD has a special plan for Israel. He wants to give her a great inheritance and make her, and all who embrace her God, joint-heirs with Jesus Christ. As joint-heirs, they would inherit with Christ all that He inherits. This includes all things seen and unseen, all that God has created. The problem is, the Devil wants to steal this inheritance for his own. This conflict is played out on earth with the small country of Israel in conflict with all other nations, as the Devil brings the nations against her.

Let us look at this wonder called Israel.

TEN TO ONE

When my boys were younger, they loved playing what they called "army men." In these make-believe battles with their miniature action figures, occasionally an argument would take place that went something like this:

ARE WE THERE YET?

"I got you—all of them!"

"You can't get all my men. You only have one man—I have ten!"

"It doesn't matter. I still got you."

"You're cheating."

"No, you don't want to admit I got you."

"You're crazy!"

"No, you're crazy, you don't play fair!"

After a few more rounds of the same, one of them eventually quits the game, leaves the room, or calls for mom or dad.

In my boys' world of make-believe, such scenarios were most often not acceptable. However, in the real world history of Israel, it is not unusual for the odds to be stacked against them and they come out victorious.[186] We only need to recall the account of Gideon with three hundred men defeating over one hundred thirty-five thousand Midianites[187] or Deborah with ten thousand soldiers defeating the Canaanite army of over one hundred thousand warriors and nine hundred chariots.[188] In our own time, when Israel regained her statehood in 1948, her neighbors did not agree with this decision. In response, Egypt, Transjordan (now Jordan), Syria, Lebanon, Iraq, and other Arab forces joined with the Arabs living in Palestine to wage war against the Jews. Israel

---

[186] Watch the YouTube video, "Miracles God performed in Israel Against All Odds."
[187] Judges 7
[188] Judges 4:6-7, 5

Appendix A: Against All Odds

was outnumbered ten to one while the whole world watched, certain that Israel would be wiped out against such odds. However, against all odds, the war ended with the Jews reclaiming Israel after over twenty-five hundred years. Present day Israel was reborn against all odds.

Notice the following statements of Israel's neighbors in the following significant conflicts.

Before the war of Independence in 1948, Arab League Secretary-General Azzam Pasha confidently declared: "This will be a war of extermination and a momentous massacre which will be spoken of like the Mongolian massacres and the Crusades."[189] Yet, being outnumbered by more than ten to one, Israel reclaimed her statehood.

Before the Six-Day War in 1967, Egyptian President Gamal Abdel Nasser let the world know: "Our basic objective will be the destruction of Israel."[190] Yet, being outnumbered by almost two to one, Israel reclaimed Jerusalem as her capital after almost two thousand years.

Before the Yom Kipper War in 1973, Libyan President Mohammar Qadaffi arrogantly broadcasted: "The battle with Israel must be such that, after it, Israel will cease to exist."[191] Yet, being outnumbered by more than twelve to one, Israel survived such a massive assault on her defenses and pushed back the nations that had initially broken through.

Even though much hostility and aggression is thrown at Israel, her neighbors have not been able to achieve their goal of removing this tiny nation and her people from the face of

---

[189] Eli E. Hertz, "Israel's Major Wars," mythsandfacts.org, 2009.
[190] Ibid.
[191] Ibid.

the earth. The big question is why? How could this be possible?

TWO MORE WONDERS

Another wonder concerning Israel was observed by Charles Krauthammer, writer for the Weekly Standard:[192]

> "Israel is the very embodiment of Jewish continuity: It is the only nation on earth that inhabits the same land, bears the same name, speaks the same language, and worships the same God that it did 3,000 years ago. You dig the soil and you find pottery from Davidic times, coins from Bar Kokhba, and 2,000-year-old scrolls written in a script remarkably like the one that today advertises ice cream at the corner candy store."

Against all odds, Israel has maintained its national and cultural identity, even though scattered and mingled with other cultures and nations—a feat no other nation has achieved. Again, the question is why? How could this be possible?

Perhaps the greatest wonder is that Israel is only slightly larger than the state of New Jersey, yet it command's the attention of world leaders and policy makers due to the continual conflict she has with her neighboring countries. Take a look at the following map to get a bird's eye view of how small Israel is compared to her hostile Islamic neighbors. Israel is the tiny, black sliver toward the lower left of the map. When these nations form a coalition against

---

[192] Charles Krauthammer, "At Last, Zion," WeeklyStandard.com," May 11, 1998.

Appendix A: Against All Odds

Israel, as they often do, it is truly a formidable force, greatly outnumbering Israel's military.

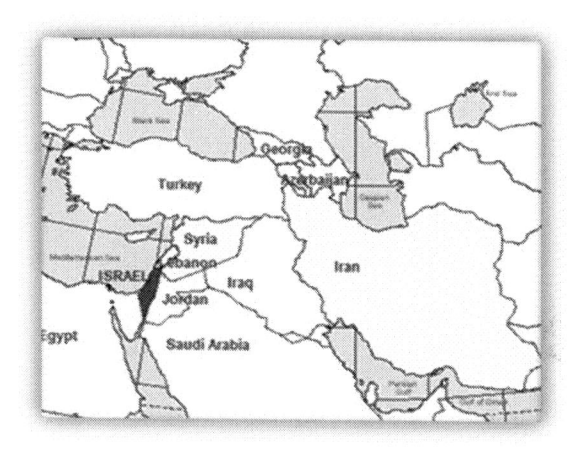

Sometimes, I try to relate to Israel by comparing her to the state of New Jersey and imagine the world's leaders making policy because of it, and that all of her neighbors (New York, Vermont, New Hampshire, Massachusetts, Connecticut, Rhode Island, Maine, Pennsylvania, Maryland, Virginia, and West Virginia) were in constant conflict with her, determined to completely wipe New Jersey off the face of the earth—zilch, kaput, no more existence!

I would end up smiling at the ridiculousness of New Jersey actually being able to defend herself and not be wiped out, even if heavily armed. I end up being totally amazed that Israel is still in existence, let alone commanding the attention of world leaders. Yet this is what is being played out with Israel since reclaiming her statehood in 1948. Again, the question is why? How is it possible for such a small, in many ways insignificant, nation to be such a powerful force against her aggressors?

GOD'S COUNTRY

My wife and I live in a rural setting with the foothills of the Allegheny Mountains spreading west to east to the south of us. Often, we look over the beauty of the area and exclaim how we live in "God's Country," especially on those days when the sun enhances the natural coloring of God's creation. Certainly, all belongs to God, but as we read Scripture, it doesn't take long to realize that Israel is favored by God above all nations and is the only nation in our present age that God claims as His. In every sense, Israel is truly God's country.

Scripture is clear that God specifically chose Israel to be His own:

> "For you are an holy people unto the Lord your God: the Lord your God has chosen you to be a special people unto himself, above all people that are upon the face of the earth."[193]

When God chose Israel, He did not choose the nation with the greatest number of people: He chose the nation with the least number.[194] Neither did He choose that nation that would be the most cooperative to His wishes: they were the most stubborn and stiff-necked of people.[195] God chose that

---

[193] Deuteronomy 7:6
[194] Deuteronomy 7:7
[195] Ezekiel 32:9, 33:3, 34:9

Appendix A: Against All Odds

nation most incapable of demonstrating great exploits on the world scene in order to demonstrate His presence and power to the world.[196]

God is not in the business of choosing those to whom the world can look at and say, "Their achievements and exploits came through their own skills." He takes those whom the world may look upon as foolish and weak to show His power. In this way He is able to reveal His wisdom and strength. The Apostle Paul speaks of this in 1 Corinthians 1:26-29:

> "For ye see your calling, brethren, how that not many wise men after the flesh, not many mighty, not many noble, are called: But God has chosen the foolish things of the world to confound the wise; and God has chosen the weak things of the world to confound the things which are mighty; And base things of the world, and things which are despised, has God chosen, yes, and things which are not, to bring to nought things that are: That no flesh should glory in his presence."

It would be around this tiny, insignificant nation that the history of the world would revolve to lead our present age into the age of the Antichrist and finally into God's kingdom where God's people become kings and joint-heirs with Christ.

Not only did God choose a people for Himself, He also chose the specific piece of real estate He would call His own. As we understand that, out of all the earth, there is one small parcel of land that God did not permit the Devil to have

---

[196] Isaiah 43:10-13

complete authority over as the god of this world,[197] we begin to comprehend the scope of the Devil's greed. The Devil is given authority over all nations except this one—and it is the most cherished out of all the nations on earth. Whoever controls Israel and Jerusalem is God of the entire created universe. Israel is God's city. David's throne is the throne that Christ will sit upon for eternity as God. The great battle of the ages revolves around this desire to sit upon God's throne in God's city.

This desire of the Devil was first seen in Isaiah 14:13, 14 when he proclaimed:

> "I will ascend into heaven, I will exalt my throne above the stars of God: I will sit also upon the mount of the congregation, in the sides of the north: I will ascend above the heights of the clouds; I will be like the most High."

The Devil's desire also is seen in the Antichrist's final conflict when he thought he gained control over God's throne when he planted "the tabernacles of his palace between the seas in the glorious holy mountain"[198] Yet, the Devil does not gain control and comes to his end.

As he operates on the concept that the strong shall inherit the earth, the Devil continually gathers earth's forces against Israel. Eventually, he will surround Israel with a coalition of nations with odds that may be a hundred to one or greater; they will certainly be much greater than anything

---

[197] 2 Corinthians 4:4; Matthew 4:8-10; John 12:31; Ephesians 2:2
[198] Daniel 11:45

Appendix A: Against All Odds

we've seen so far. In this final battle, God will show His strength as Israel stands strong and her aggressors fall.[199]

Out of all nations, Israel is the land God chose to care for and to watch over as recorded in Deuteronomy 11:12:

> "A land which the Lord your God cares for: the eyes of the Lord your God are always upon it, from the beginning of the year even unto the end of the year."

It is this protective care that has guided Israel toward victory in her military campaigns, even though the odds were greatly against her. It is this protective care that has kept Israel nationally and culturally pure throughout the generations, regardless of the culture they were in. It is this protective care that will ensure that even though she will experience many troubles and wars and many victories and defeats, Israel will never be wiped off the face of the earth. It is Israel's destiny to inherit all that God has created as joint-heirs with His Son, Jesus Christ—and God will see to it that she does.

JOINT HEIRS

God chose Israel not because she was capable of the miraculous exploits that has earmarked her history, but to reveal His power and greatness. Israel is God's witness to show everyone in all nations who He is.[200] Yet, God's plan for Israel is much more inclusive than just Israel. His plan includes drawing to Him everyone who will recognize Him

---

199 Revelation 20:7-10
200 Isaiah 43:10

and receive His wonderful plan to make them rulers with Him over the trillions times trillions of galaxies that are within the universe. God has created you and me to become "joint-heirs" with the Jews through Jesus Christ, meaning that everything that belongs to Jesus will also belong to us.[201] Pause for a moment from your reading. Look in the mirror. Now introduce yourself to a king in training[202] who will rule with Christ over all that He has created. I have to admit, I find all this absolutely mind-blowing, but I find it amazingly true.

This great plan of God is still in its infancy. It began a little over six thousand years ago when God put into existence the entire material universe and created a new creature called man. Man was God's greatest creation, greater than the angels. Man was the only creature with God's Spirit living within them, created to be a king, and created to rule over all God's creation as joint heirs with His Son.

After creating the material universe, His next step was the creation of kings and priests to rule over this vast, ever expanding expanse. Once the rulers are in place, He would then continue His promise to Abraham, Isaac, and Jacob to make their children and their children's children as numberless as the stars in the sky and the grains of sand along the shores. Apparently, this new creation will populate the galaxies, seeing as the earth would not be able to hold so many people.

---

201 Romans 8:17; Hebrews 1:2
202 For a brief study concerning the training God puts us through to be His children and kings in His kingdom, see Appendix E.

Appendix A: Against All Odds

Consider it in this way: Go to a beach and stop at a place of your choosing. Look down at all the grains of sand below you; then look up and down the beach at the miles of sand just like what you're standing on, then consider all the hundreds of beaches that are throughout the world with innumerable number of grains of sand. This must be how God sees the trillions times trillions of galaxies with their trillions times trillions of stars. Over all this, you are being trained now to be joint-heirs with Jesus Christ. Let me sit down for a moment before I faint, while you take a second look in the mirror at a future king who will rule all this with Jesus Christ.

IN CLOSING

As we read Scripture, it quickly becomes clear that Israel is a special people to God. Because of this relationship, and God's ownership over this one small parcel of land, the Devil strives to destroy Israel and take possession of the land. In his efforts, he uses the nations of the earth to come against her to steal her inheritance for his own.[203]

The timelines we look at in this book reveal those empires the Devil raises up to organize the nations that will oppress and persecute Israel. Eventually, he will muster the forces of the nations to war against Israel, building odds that can only be speculated to be at one hundred to one or greater in the Devil's favor. Despite that, Israel will not be wiped out as God intervenes to prepare Israel to receive her eternal inheritance.

---

203 Matthew 21:33-39

ARE WE THERE YET?

Appendix B
God of This World

GOD OWNS THE EARTH, BUT THE DEVIL IS GIVEN AUTHORITY TO EXERT HIS WILL OVER THE EARTH

NO ONE SHOULD BE SURPRISED BY THIS STATEMENT. Jesus admitted that His kingdom was some place not on this earth and that this earth is under the authority of someone else when He answered Pilate:

> "My kingdom is not of this world: if my kingdom were of this world, then would my servants fight, that I should not be delivered to the Jews: but now is my kingdom not from hence."[204]

The Apostle Paul also confirms the Devil's authority when he wrote to the Corinthians:

> "But if our gospel be hid, it is hid to them that are lost: In whom the god of this world has blinded the minds of them which believe not, lest the light of the glorious gospel of Christ, who is the image of God, should shine unto them."[205]

---

204 John 18:36
205 2 Corinthians 4:3, 4

ARE WE THERE YET?

The Devil's purpose on earth is to deceive[206] everyone he can to depart from trusting in God and to instead trust in everything that is in the world. He is continually prowling to and fro in the earth looking for those he can destroy.[207] He is our true enemy,[208] not the people and situations that rise up against us.[209]

How does the Devil tempt us, seeking to move us from God's eternal inheritance?

The Devil uses the whole world against us: "The whole world lies in wickedness."[210] Because we live in righteousness and not wickedness, the world hates us and comes against us. John 15:18, 19 confirms this sentiment:

> "If the world hate you, ye know that it hated me before it hated you. If ye were of the world, the world would love his own: but because ye are not of the world, but I have chosen you out of the world, therefore the world hates you."

The world, and everything in it, is identified as everything that appeals to our body, everything that can be seen with our eyes, and everything that gives us a sense of pride, self-importance, conceit, or arrogance about our life.[211] It is all that is within the world that we are to separate our affections from. If we don't, then the love of God is not in us since we cannot love both the things of the world and the

---

206 2 Corinthians 4:3, 4; Revelation 12:9
207 1 Peter 5:8
208 1 Peter 5:8
209 Ephesians 6:11,12
210 1 John 5:19
211 1 John 2:16

Appendix B: God of this World

things of God.[212] This is a great battle we are in, especially since "the whole world lies in wickedness."[213] Yet it is a battle we must fight. It is a battle you can win.

This great battle is between the things of this world and the things of God. To not be overcome by the world, we must keep our focus on the things above where Christ and our real home are:

> "If ye then be risen with Christ, seek those things which are above, where Christ sits on the right hand of God. Set your affection on things above, not on things on the earth. For ye are dead, and your life is hid with Christ in God."[214]

We are to live as pilgrims and strangers who live temperately with the world until we reach our eternal home.[215] Truly, this world is not our home. We are to relate to the things of this world in a disciplined, temperate way, using what is in the world to maintain our existence without abusing what the world offers.[216]

As our enemy, the Devil is a sly old fox who uses every ploy he can throw at us. He will use the dark and dastardly, as well as the good and pleasant to snag us into his web. It was not the dark, evil, or distasteful that caused the entire world to be corrupted with sin. Eve was deceived with what was "good for food," "pleasant to the eyes," and with what

---

212 1 John 2:15; Matthew 6:24
213 1 John 5:19
214 Colossians 3:1-3
215 1 Peter 2:11-17
216 1 Corinthians 7:29-31

would "make her wise."[217] This is all that is in the world as described by the Apostle John: the lust of the flesh, the lust of the eyes, and the pride of life.

Whether it is the dark and dastardly or the good and pleasant, the Devil doesn't tempt us with what does not appeal to us, but with what does appeal. For someone who claims the name of Christ, this might be the works and practices that a Christian is involved in. Jesus and the Apostle Paul warned that apostasy would become so great that the majority claiming the name of Christ will not belong to Christ.[218] They will be Christians without the Holy Spirit, which means they are not Christian at all. As we read in Revelation chapters two and three, good Christian works, correct doctrine, and martyrdom does not make us Christian. What makes us Christian is the Holy Spirit within us.[219] Apostasy is a departure from the Holy Spirit, not always a departure from good works or correct doctrine.

All that is within the world is the nature of the Devil. After he was given authority over the earth, he began creating a world after his own nature. The Devil's nature is outlined for us in Ezekiel 28:12-19[220]:

> "Son of man, take up a lamentation upon the king of Tyrus, and say unto him, Thus says the Lord God; You seal up the sum, full of wisdom, and perfect in beauty.

---

217 Genesis 3:6
218 Matthew 25:1-30; 2 Thessalonians 2:3; 2 Timothy 3:5; Revelation 2 & 3
219 Romans 8:9
220 We know this king Tyrus is referring to the Devil because of the description referring to him as "the anointed cherub" and not an actual king on earth.

Appendix B: God of this World

You have been in Eden the garden of God; every precious stone was your covering, the sardius, topaz, and the diamond, the beryl, the onyx, and the jasper, the sapphire, the emerald, and the carbuncle, and gold: the workmanship of your tabrets and of your pipes was prepared in you in the day that you was created. You are the anointed cherub that covers; and I have set you so: you was upon the holy mountain of God; you have walked up and down in the midst of the stones of fire. You was perfect in your ways from the day that you was created, till iniquity was found in you. By the multitude of your merchandise they have filled the midst of you with violence, and you have sinned: therefore I will cast you as profane out of the mountain of God: and I will destroy you, O covering cherub, from the midst of the stones of fire. Your heart was lifted up because of your beauty, you have corrupted your wisdom by reason of your brightness: I will cast you to the ground, I will lay you before kings, that they may behold you. You have defiled your sanctuaries by the multitude of your iniquities, by the iniquity of your traffic; therefore will I bring forth a fire from the midst of you, it shall devour you, and I will bring you to ashes upon the earth in the sight of all them that behold you. All they that know you among the people shall be astonished at you: you shall be a terror, and never shall you be any more."

To outline the Devil's focus when he was in heaven, and which he is now creating on earth, we find he was *full of wisdom, perfect in beauty, loved possessions, loved to do business deceptively, and was musical*. This nature and focus of the Devil is without question the world's focus. Knowledge, wisdom, beauty, possessions, business, and music are placed on high pedestals in this life.

As the god of this world, the Devil has authority to use knowledge, wisdom, beauty, possessions, our business

ARE WE THERE YET?

activity, and music to tempt us to move from security in God to find security in what can be seen and accomplished by man. Because of this battle, God refers to the business people and bankers as *sorcerers*.[221]

When I first realized that sorcerers and business people were placed in the same boat, paddling the same oars, I was puzzled since my concept of a sorcerer was of a man with a long beard standing in the center of a circle in a dimly lit room invoking demons with arcane incantations. When I realized the Devil's nature was broader than what we've been conditioned to believe and had to do with taking our focus off God and placing it upon those things belonging to the world, it all made sense. The goal of the business world is to entice us to buy their products with claims that our health, wealth, and happiness can be found in their product. The business world is redirecting our faith from God whether they understand that or not. In this way, the entire world is being conditioned to align with the Devil's agenda.

The focus the Devil establishes on earth was the cause of his fall in heaven. Ezekiel tells us his fall came 1) because his many possessions filled him with violence and sin.[222] 2) His heart was filled with great pride because of his beauty.[223] 3) His wisdom was corrupted because he took great pride in his intellect,[224] and 4) his dwelling places were ruined

---

221 Revelation 18:23
222 Ezekiel 28:16
223 Ezekiel 28:17a
224 Ezekiel 28:17b

Appendix B: God of this World

because of his deceptive business practices.[225] The Devil's goal is to tempt you to follow his path.

The Devil has created a world system that makes it easy for you to depart God's plan for health, wealth, and happiness for his own plan. Lucifer loved the things he possessed in heaven, had great greed, and would sin to gain more until his pride grew so great that he thought he could actually take God's place and have it all.[226] This is the kind of world the Devil creates on earth. This is the great battle of the ages: to trust in God or to trust the things that are in the world. What do you trust? Is it paychecks, people, and pleasure? The ultimate test of our faith will come when the Antichrist mandates the entire world to accept his cashless, economic system or face losing it all, going to prison, or facing death.

Matthew 6:19-34 is a good passage to read until it sinks in deep and becomes an engrafted part of your life. It speaks of this great battle and encourages us not to worry about even the essentials for living: food in the cupboard, drink on the table, clothes on our back. If there were any earthly thing that should worry us, it would be these, right? Wrong! This passage helps us to understand that nothing should keep us from God's peace, no matter how uncertain our situation becomes.

The Devil's world, the one we live in now, works hard to deceive and tell us that we should focus on and depend on the things of earth, but God speaks differently. As the world encourages us to focus on working to eliminate poverty, to

---

225 Ezekiel 28:18
226 Isaiah 14:12-14

end all war, to achieve global peace, to eliminate every disease, to stop ethnic injustices, and to find harmony among religions, Jesus is clear in Matthew 24 that these will never be done away with and will continue to increase until His return. We live at a time when there are more organizations and people seeking to overcome these ills than at any other time in history, yet the result has not been their decrease, but continual increase.

This is just another ploy of the Devil to divert you from trusting in God by getting you to focus on great and noble humanitarian causes. Don't take me wrong; we are to take care of one another and are encouraged to do so, but to put forth great amounts of energy to eradicate or stop any of these is absolutely fruitless, just another diversion from the things belonging to God. My goal is to take care of those I see eyeball to eyeball and hang out elbow to elbow with.

WHO DO YOU TRUST? GOD OR THEWORLD?

Soon the age of the Antichrist will be here. These days will be filled with great pressure so that even the strongest of Christians will be tempted to depart their faith by trusting what the world offers.[227] These days will be so without faith that Jesus asks the question in Luke 18:8: "Nevertheless when the Son of man comes, shall he find faith on the earth?" Reread Luke 18:1-8 to discover for yourself what Jesus considers to be the key element of faith. Then ask yourself, based upon Jesus' definition of faith, "Do I truly have faith?" If

---

227 Matthew 24:24

Appendix B: God of this World

you do not easily find this key, go to Appendix D and read, "The Key to Faith."

DISTRIBUTION CENTERS

In order to spread his message about possessions, beauty, and wisdom, the Devil needs distribution centers to pour out his nature upon the earth. This is one of the purposes of nations. The main empires raised up for this purpose are found in our prophetic timeline. This system the Devil has created for our world is called "Mystery Babylon."[228]

In Revelation 17, Mystery Babylon is described as a woman sitting "upon a scarlet colored beast, full of names of blasphemy, having seven heads and ten horns."[229] The beast with seven heads and ten horns are the nations and kings of the earth. It is through these that Mystery Babylon distributes her "abominations and fornications."[230] These originate from within her and is the reason she is called "the mother of harlots and abominations of the earth."[231]

To understand the nature of the Devil is to understand why we are called to "love not the world," to "fast," to "deny ourselves," to "focus on the things above," and to "seek first the kingdom of God and His righteousness." These are not nice sentiments...but are weapons of warfare to fight the battle between the things of this world and the things of God.

---

[228] Revelation 17:3-5
[229] Revelation 17:3
[230] Revelation 17:4
[231] Revelation 17:5

ARE WE THERE YET?

God has given specific disciplines to overcome the world's attacks on our body, mind, and spirit. He gives fasting and temperance for our body,[232] single mindedness and thinking on the things above and things pure for the mind,[233] and prayer, walking in God's Spirit, and seeking righteousness for our spirit.[234] Also, Ephesians 6:11-18 gives a detailed description of the armor we are to put on. It cannot be emphasized enough that this world is getting tougher to be a Christian in and if we don't do it God's way, there just may not be any hope for you or me. Having our armor in good working order is not an option. Here's the armor listed in Ephesians:

> "Put on the whole armor of God, that ye may be able to stand against the wiles of the devil. For we wrestle not against flesh and blood, but against principalities, against powers, against the rulers of the darkness of this world, against spiritual wickedness in high places.
>
> Wherefore take unto you the whole armor of God, that ye may be able to withstand in the evil day, and having done all, to stand. Stand therefore, having your loins girt about with truth, and having on the breastplate of righteousness; And your feet shod with the preparation of the gospel of peace; Above all, taking the shield of faith, wherewith ye shall be able to quench all the fiery darts of the wicked. And take the helmet of salvation, and the sword of the Spirit, which is the word of God: Praying always with all prayer and supplication in the Spirit, and watching thereunto with all perseverance and supplication for all saints;"

---

232 Matthew 6:16; 1 Corinthians 9:25
233 Luke 18:1-8; Matthew 6:22; Colossians 3:2; Philippians 4:6-9
234 Galatians 5:19-25; Matthew 6:33

Appendix B: God of this World

The Devil may have authority over this world, but God owns it. The day is soon coming when the Devil will be evicted, and you and I will take possession over all that the Devil claims.[235] In the meantime, hold on just a little while longer...it won't be long.

---

[235] Daniel 7:21,22

ARE WE THERE YET?

Appendix C
Daniel 11 Commentary

THE AMPLIFIED BIBLE (AMP) ADDS MUCH HISTORICAL REFERENCES TO THE BIBLICAL NARRATIVE. I ADD IT HERE FOR THIS REASON. I HAVE ADDED HEADINGS TO GIVE direction.

ALEXANDER THE GREAT (11:1-4)

"Also I, in the first year of Darius the Mede, I (Gabriel) arose to be an encouragement and a protection for him. ² And now I will tell you the truth. Behold, three more kings are going to arise in Persia. Then a fourth will become far richer than all of them. When he becomes strong through his riches he will stir up the whole *empire* against the realm of Greece. ³ Then a mighty [warlike, threatening] king will arise who will rule with great authority and do as he pleases. ⁴ But as soon as he (Alexander) has risen, his kingdom will be broken [by his death] and divided toward the four winds of heaven [the north, south, east, and west], but not to his descendants, nor according to the [Grecian] authority with which he ruled, for his kingdom will be torn out *and* uprooted and given to others (his four generals) to the exclusion of these.

NORTHERN AND SOUTHERN KINGS (11:5-19)

5 "Then the king of the South (Egypt) will be strong, along with one of his princes who will be stronger than he and have dominance over him; his domain will be a great dominion. 6 After some years the Syrian king of the North and the Egyptian king of the South will make an alliance; the daughter (Berenice) of the king of the South will come to the king of the North to make an equitable *and* peaceful agreement (marriage); but she will not retain the power of her position, nor will he retain his power. She will be handed over with her attendants and her father as well as he who supported her in those times. 7 But out of a branch of her [familial] roots will one (her brother, Ptolemy III Euergetes I) arise in his place, and he will come against the [Syrian] army and enter the fortress of the king of the North, and he will deal with them and will prevail. 8 Also he will carry off to Egypt their [Syrian] gods with their cast images and their precious *and* costly treasure of silver and of gold, and he will refrain from waging war against the king of the North for some years. 9 And the king of the North will come into the realm of the king of the South, but he will retreat to his own country [badly defeated].

10 "His sons will prepare for battle and assemble a multitude of great forces; which will keep on coming and overflow [the land], and pass through, so that they may again

Appendix C: Daniel 11 Commentary

wage war as far as his fortress. **11** The king of the South (Ptolemy IV Philopator of Egypt) will be enraged and go out and fight with the king of the North (Antiochus III the Great); and [i]the Syrian king will raise a great multitude (army), but the multitude shall be given into the hand of the *Egyptian king*. **12** When the multitude (army) is captured *and* carried away, the heart of the *Egyptian king* will be proud (arrogant), and he will cause tens of thousands to fall, but he will not prevail. **13** For the king of the North will again raise a multitude (army) greater than the one before, and after several years he will advance with a great army and substantial equipment.

14 "In those times many will rise up against the king of the South (Egypt); also the violent men among your own people will arise in order to fulfill the [earlier] visions, but they will fail. **15** Then the king of the North (Syria) will come and build up siege ramps and capture a well-fortified city. The forces of the South will not stand *their ground*, not even the finest troops, for there will be no strength to stand [against the Syrian king]. **16** But he (Syria) who comes against him (Egypt) will do exactly as he pleases, and no one will be able to stand against him; he (Antiochus III the Great) will also stay for a time in the Beautiful *and* Glorious Land [of Israel], with destruction in his hand. **17** He will be determined to come with the power of his entire kingdom, and propose equitable conditions *and* terms of peace, which he will put into effect [by making an agreement with the king of the South]. He will also give him his daughter (Cleopatra I), *in an attempt* to overthrow the kingdom, but it will not succeed or be to his advantage. **18** After this, he (Antiochus III the Great,

ARE WE THERE YET?

King of Syria) will turn his attention to the[l] islands *and* coastlands and capture many [of them]. But a commander (Lucius Scipio Asiaticus of Rome) will put an end to his aggression [toward Rome's territorial interests]; in fact, he will repay his insolence *and* turn his audacity back upon him. ¹⁹ Then he will turn back toward the fortresses of his own land [of Syria], but he will stumble and fall and not be found.

ANTIOCHUS IV EPIPHANES (11:20-35)

²⁰ "Then in his place one (his eldest son, Seleucus IV Philopator) will arise who will send an oppressor through the Jewel of his kingdom; yet within a few days he will be shattered, though not in anger nor in battle. ²¹ And in his place [in Syria] will arise a despicable *and* despised person, to whom royal majesty *and* the honor of kingship have not been conferred, but he will come [without warning] in a time of tranquility and seize the kingdom by intrigue. ²² The overwhelming forces [of the invading armies of Egypt] will be flooded away before him *and* smashed; and also the [o]prince of the covenant [will be smashed]. ²³ After an [p]alliance is made with him he will work deceitfully, and he will go up and gain power with a small *force of* people. ²⁴ In a time of tranquility, [without warning] he will enter the most productive *and* richest parts of the kingdom [of Egypt], and he will accomplish that which his fathers never did, nor his fathers' fathers; he will distribute plunder, spoil and goods among them. He will devise plans against strongholds, but only for a time [decreed by God]. ²⁵ He will

Appendix C: Daniel 11 Commentary

stir up his strength and courage against [his former Egyptian ally] the king of the South (Ptolemy VI) with a great army; so the king of the South will prepare an extremely great and powerful army to wage war, but he will not stand, for schemes will be devised against him. 26 Yes, those who eat his fine food will betray *and* destroy him (Ptolemy VI), and his army will be swept away, and many will fall down slain. 27 And as for both of these [a]kings, their hearts will be set on doing evil; they will speak lies over the same table, but it will not succeed, for the end is yet to come at the appointed time. 28 Then he (Antiochus IV Epiphanes) will return to his land with great treasure (plunder); and his heart will be set against the holy covenant, and he will take action and return to his own land (Syria).

29 "At the time appointed [by God] he will return and come into the South, but this last time will not be successful as were the previous invasions [of Egypt]. 30 For ships of Cyprus [in Roman hands] will come against him; therefore he will be discouraged and turn back [to Israel] and carry out his rage against the holy covenant and take action; so he will return and show favoritism toward those [Jews] who abandon (break) the holy covenant [with God]. 31 Armed forces of his will arise [in Jerusalem] and defile *and* desecrate the sanctuary, the [spiritual] stronghold, and will do away with the regular sacrifice [that is, the daily burnt offering]; and they will set up [a pagan altar in the sanctuary which is] the abomination of desolation. 32 With smooth *words* [of flattery and praise] he will turn to godlessness those who [are willing to] disregard the [Mosaic] covenant, but the people who [are spiritually mature and] know their God will

display strength and take action [to resist]. ³³ They who are wise *and* have spiritual insight among the people will instruct many *and* help them understand; yet for many days some [of them and their followers] will fall by the sword and by flame, by captivity and by plunder. ³⁴ Now when they fall they will receive a little help, and many will join with them in hypocrisy. ³⁵ Some of those who are [spiritually] wise *and* have insight will fall [as martyrs] in order to refine, to purge and to make those among God's people pure, until the end time; because it is yet to come at the time appointed [by God].

THE ANTICHRIST (11:36-45)

³⁶ "Then the [r]king (the Antichrist) will do exactly as he pleases; he will exalt himself and magnify himself above every god and will speak astounding *and* disgusting things against the God of gods and he will prosper until the indignation is finished, for that which is determined [by God] will be done. ³⁷ He will have no regard for the gods of his fathers or for the desire of women, nor will he have regard for any *other* god, for he shall magnify himself above them all. ³⁸ Instead, he will honor a god of fortresses, a god whom his fathers did not know; he will honor him with gold and silver, with precious stones and with expensive things. ³⁹ He will act against the strongest fortresses with *the help of* a foreign god; he will give great honor to those who acknowledge him and he will cause them to rule over the many, and will parcel out land for a price.

Appendix C: Daniel 11 Commentary

⁴⁰ "At the end time the king of the South will push *and* attack him (the Antichrist), and the king of the North will storm against him with chariots and horsemen and with many ships; and he will enter countries, overwhelm them and pass through. ⁴¹ He shall also enter the Beautiful *and* Glorious Land (Israel), and many countries will fall, but these will be rescued out of his hand: Edom, Moab, and the foremost [core] of the people of Ammon. ⁴² Then he will stretch out his hand against other countries, but Egypt will not be among the ones which escape. ⁴³ He will have power over the treasures of gold and silver and over all the precious things of Egypt, and the Libyans and the Ethiopians *will follow* in his footsteps. ⁴⁴ But rumors from the east and from the north will alarm *and* disturb him, and he will set out with great fury to destroy and to annihilate many. ⁴⁵ He will pitch his palatial tents between the seas and the glorious Holy Mountain (Zion); yet he will come to his end with no one to help him [in his final battle with God].

ARE WE THERE YET?

Appendix D
The Key to Faith

IF YOU HAVEN'T ALREADY, TAKE A MOMENT TO READ LUKE 18:1-8. LEAVE YOUR BIBLE OPEN AS WE LOOK AT THIS PARABLE. FIRST NOTICE HOW LUKE PREFACES THE parable of the persistent widow with:

> "And he spoke a parable unto them to this end, that men ought always to pray, and not to faint;"[236]

Luke then records the words of Jesus telling of a persistent widow who repeatedly requested a judge to avenge her of her adversary. She kept coming and coming to the judge until he gave in to her request.[237] Jesus then poses the following question:

> "And shall not God avenge his own elect, which cry day and night unto him, though he bear long with them?"[238]

---

[236] Luke 18:1
[237] Luke 18:3
[238] Luke 18:7

ARE WE THERE YET?

This also is an obvious statement concerning prayer, but then notice what Jesus says in the very next and last verse of the parable:

> "Nevertheless when the Son of man comes, shall he find faith on the earth?"[239]

Did you catch that? Luke tells us the parable is about prayer.[240] Jesus confirms that it is about prayer,[241] yet Jesus ends the parable speaking about faith.[242] Why? Apparently the emphasis is on the inseparableness of prayer and faith. If you have faith, you pray. If you pray, you have faith. The key element of faith is prayer, talking with an actual God. Do you take time to talk with God? When Jesus returns, will He find you to be a man or woman who communicates with His Father?

---

[239] Luke 18:8
[240] Luke 18:1
[241] Luke 18:7
[242] Luke 18:8

Appendix E
Kings in Training

THE CURRICULUM FOR TRAINING ETERNAL KINGS CONSISTS OF ONE SUBJECT: FAITH IN GOD.

IT SEEMS SIMPLE ENOUGH, BUT THE DIFFICULTY comes in not trying to become emotionally or mentally attached to anything in life that can be seen, felt, and taken pleasure in. Future kings are to find their hope and pleasure in the promises given to them by God. These promises include receiving an eternal inheritance, being joint heirs with Christ, receiving eternal life, and living in the very physical presence of God.

The fulfillment of these promises is in an unseen future, whereas life on earth can be felt, experienced, and taken pleasure in now. This is where the conflict enters: to give up what is before us for what we cannot see. We are called to follow Abraham's faith, to pack up all, and travel toward an inheritance we have not seen, but is promised to us by God.[243]

Scripture is clear that everything of earth is not of God and belongs to the world.[244] The things of God are not in or of this world. Our hope and life are in God's future promises

---

243 Hebrews 11:8-10
244 1 John 2:16

ARE WE THERE YET?

and of an eternal home of far more value than anything this world might offer. This is such a treasure that once we discern its value and reality, we will gladly give up all this world has to offer to receive it, including our life if necessary.[245]

One of the reasons we detach ourselves from the things of this world is because all that can be seen is developed after the Devil's nature. The Devil is the god of this world. His goal is to create a world after his image, which is to focus on possessions, beauty, riches, and pride in what one has.[246] In the negative, his focus is greed, pride, and power. It was this focus that caused Lucifer to sin to the point that he desired and thought he could take God's place.[247] It is this focus that God is training His future kings not to hold onto or trust in—even if it is the physical necessities to sustain life.[248] Our goal is to use the things of this world to get through life, but without attachment to or pride or greed for them.[249] The Devil uses all things in the world—even Christian things—to detour us from being single minded toward the great inheritance that will be ours.

FAITH TRAINING

To train us in faith and detachment from the world, God raised up Abraham to be our example. Through Abraham, God laid the foundation for faith and showed what faith looks

---

245 Matthew 13:44-46
246 Ezekiel 28:14-19 See also Appendix B
247 Isaiah 14:13-14
248 Matthew 6:24-34
249 1 Corinthians 7:31

Appendix E: Kings in Training

like. What faith looked like was a continual giving up of the things of this world for a promise that many times did not look as if it were going to happen. In the following paragraphs, I have outlined six faith teachings that strengthened Abraham's faith and that would be the foundation stones for our own faith.

FAITH TEACHING ONE: ABRAHAM BELIEVED GOD BEFORE GOD SPOKE TO HIM [250]

Abraham would have heard the stories about Adam and Eve and Noah and the Flood directly from Shem, the son of Noah, who was alive for 150 years of Abraham's life. To Abraham, these stories were not far distant stories of people in a far away land that he didn't know; they were his story...his family history, and would have been the spark for Abraham wanting to please this God that he heard about, but never knew in the same way that Adam or Noah had. Before God revealed himself personally to Abraham, Abraham's desire was to please this God by living righteously.

Before God reveals Himself to us, we also must have the desire to want to know God and to please Him. There must be something within us that reaches out to God in such a strong way that we are willing to give up everything we have and are just to have God with us.[251] We must be like the woman who searches her entire house, sweeping every nook and

---

[250] A big thanks goes out to Steve Teets for his insights into this first faith teaching. I originally had five until Steve shared his insights with our Bible Study group. Now I have six.
[251] Matthew 13:45, 46 The Pearl of Great Price

cranny until she finds her lost coin.[252] If there is no desire for God, there will be no finding of God. If we do not find God, we cannot put our faith and trust in the One we do not know.

FAITH TEACHING TWO: ABRAHAM HEARD GOD'S VOICE

If this teaching is not grasped, embraced, and entered into, none of the faith teachings we look at will matter. Abraham's faith was not based only upon intellect, decisiveness, or impressions of what he thought was God's direction or will. Abraham's faith was based upon hearing the audible voice of God. It was this "voice"[253] that he obeyed,[254] not an impression, not an "I think God wants me to...", not an indecisiveness between "two" wills of God. There was an audible voice that Abraham heard, followed, and communicated with. When Jesus came, He also relates that those who belong to Him also "hear" His voice.[255]

We don't have to wonder if we hear God, we can know without a doubt because God is actual—He is real. What about those statements many make about "God told me to..." or "God wanted me to...."? Did God really speak? Did you really obey?

---

252 Luke 5:8-10
253 Genesis 12:1, 7; 13:14; 15:1,4,7,13; 17:1,3,9,15,19; 18:113,17,26,28-32; 21:12; 22:1-2
254 Genesis 12:4,8; 13:18; 15:10; 17:23; 22:3, 18
255 John 10:4,16,27; Hebrews 3:7; Revelation 3:20

Appendix E: Kings in Training

FAITH TEACHING THREE: ABRAHAM PACKED UP ALL THAT HE OWNED, TO TRAVEL TO A LAND HE DID NOT KNOW... ONLY BECAUSE GOD TOLD HIM TO DO IT.[256]

Abraham was seventy-five years old and had lived in Haran most of his life since moving there with his father after God confused the languages at the tower of Babel.[257] No doubt Abraham was settled and content to remain here until his death. Yet, when he heard God asking him to leave, he packed it all up and made the long, and what would become an uncertain journey toward the land God instructed him to go.

FAITH TEACHING FOUR: ABRAHAM WAS TOLD THAT HE AND HIS WIFE WOULD HAVE A BABY, THOUGH THEY WERE NINETY AND EIGHTY YEARS OLD AND PAST THE AGE OF HAVING CHILDREN.[258]

This is the first physical sign to Abraham that God would do what He had promised, though it would be impossible through any means that the world could offer. So unlikely did such a promise seem that Abraham and his wife took it into their own hands to bring forth a child through other means. Ishmael was the result of this action, yet he did not fulfill God's promise that Abraham's wife would have the child. Abraham was one hundred years of age and Sarah

---

256 Genesis 12:1-5
257 Genesis 11:7-8, 31; 10:32.
258 Genesis 15:1-7

ninety when Isaac was born from her womb. Seeing the impossible would prepare Abraham for his greatest test of faith.

FAITH TEACHING FIVE
ABRAHAM WAS TOLD TO SACRIFICE ISAAC, HIS SON OF PROMISE.[259]

The greatest treasure of any parent is their sons and daughters; that treasure increases in value when it is the fulfillment of a promise from God and given against all odds. At such a request to kill his own son, the stress Abraham felt mentally and emotionally must have been almost too much to bear. "Give up my own son? Sacrifice him with my own hands?" Yet, God spoke in an audible voice, and there was no question it was God who spoke.

No doubt Abraham weighed God's previous promise to him that his seed would be as numberless as the stars in the sky against this new request to sacrifice his son. He reasoned that God was able to raise Isaac even from the dead.[260] Abraham obeyed God, yet when the sacrificial knife was raised, ready to end Isaac's life, God intervened, sending His angel to stop him, providing a ram in Isaac's place.

Wow! What a reunion and tear-flowing event this must have been. What an establishment of faith this would be. Even God and all the angels of heaven realized the immensity of the task when the angel stated, "Now I know that you fear God, seeing you have not withheld your son, your only son

---

[259] Genesis 22:1-14
[260] Hebrews 11:17-19

Appendix E: Kings in Training

from me."[261] It was no doubt this final test which made strong and unmovable the faith that would earmark Israel's history and the faith of Christians.

FAITH TEACHING SIX
ABRAHAM OBEYED

None of the other faith teachings would matter, even hearing God's voice, if this one was not followed through with. Abraham heard. Abraham considered. Abraham obeyed.[262] In our age of walking with the actual presence of God, we are encouraged to "Take heed to the ministry which you have received in the Lord, that you fulfill it."[263] We are also warned, "Nevertheless when the Son of man comes, shall he find faith on the earth?"[264] Are you taking heed to what God has given you to do? Do you truly have faith? Do you know what faith's essential quality is? Read Luke 18:1-8 to find out.[265]

Abraham's faith may be summed up in this: the detachment from even the most cherished treasures the world can offer in favor of an inheritance that, at times, seems uncertain and even impossible to achieve.

---

261 Genesis 22:12
262 Genesis 12:4,8; 13:18; 15:10; 17:23; 22:3, 18
263 Colossians 4:17
264 Luke 18:8
265 If you did not find faith's essential quality, go to Appendix D–but don't cheat; read the Scripture and discover it for yourself.

ARE WE THERE YET?

FAITH'S GREATEST ALLY

Wouldn't it be great if faith was as easy as understanding that God is real, understanding His Word, and knowing without a doubt that He is going to fulfill what He promised? Sounds simple enough; so simple, in fact, that we've developed phrases such as "God said it, I believe it, that settles it." However, the reality is not so simple. When we look at the history of Israel and the miracles God performed for them—even the generation that witnessed the miraculous deliverance out of Egypt and God's provision in the wilderness—they still grumbled against God when things were not going as they wanted. It is obvious that seeing does not produce belief for the long haul. Seeing believes for the moment, but faith believes for an eternity.

My mother tells of the time when my grandmother lived in the "boondocks," referring to her isolated country home. At this time in her life, she had no phone, no vehicle, and lived too far from town or neighbors to walk for any needs she might have. So when she ran out of food, she had no way of taking care of her need. It was three days later that one of her daughters visited, noticed the lack of food, and asked what she had been eating...my grandmother's response? "I had nothing. God wanted me to fast these three days."

This is quite a contrast to the highly stressed, burden-filled lady who asked for prayer from her denomination because of losing her job. She admitted that she *only* had enough food and resources for a month and didn't know what she was going to do. It is a good thing to exercise our faith by asking the church to pray, but is it faith when we

Appendix E: Kings in Training

allow stress and burdens to overshadow our prayers? Do we truly trust God when we lose the peace of God?

I heard a speaker say that, "You never know whether you are truly living by faith, until you are in a situation where faith is all you have." The lady above was obviously not living according to the faith outlined in Matthew 6:34:

> "So do not worry or be anxious about tomorrow, for tomorrow will have worries and anxieties of its own. Sufficient for each day is its own trouble."[266]

All of her needs were being taken care of for that day and many days after. There was no need to let worry and stress destroy her peace with God. Obviously, she lost her peace, not because she did not have what she needed for the day, but because she was concerned about what she might not have in the following month. In contrast, my grandmother knew that, whether she had her necessities or not, God permitted what He felt was for her highest good. She chose to rest in Him instead of her physical need.

The training ground for faith is the stresses placed upon it. Most of us have no doubt heard how a body builder receives his chiseled, perfect looking physique by applying stress to his various muscles. In a similar way, we build a strong, chiseled faith by the stresses applied to it. You never know how much patience you really have until you are in a position where you must exercise patience. Indeed, you will not understand God's provision until you are in a position when you have no available resources, and neither will you

---

[266] Taken from the Amplified Version of the Bible

ARE WE THERE YET?

truly experience the peace of God until your little world has been turned upside down. James 1:1-3 is clear on this when the apostle wrote:

> "My brothers, count it all joy when ye fall into many temptations; Knowing this, that the trying of your faith works patience. But let patience have her perfect work, that ye may be perfect and entire, wanting nothing."

Amazing, isn't it? Stress develops patience and patience leads to great faith and perfection.

To train the stubborn, stiff-necked, rebellious Israel to be His people, God gave to them the example of Abraham, the father of faith, and then began to develop faith in them. The Israelites training ground for faith was through four hundred years of suffering in Egypt,[267] forty years of wanderings in the wilderness,[268] twenty-five hundred years controlled by other nations, over two thousand years without a nation, and through various wars and trials. In our present age, the Israelites still do not trust God. This will not change until the great tribulation by the Antichrist brings great destruction to her in the last of the last days. In the midst of her greatest trial, Israel will return to God, never to depart from Him again.

Did you notice the timeframe it takes to develop a people worthy to receive God's promised inheritance? We are looking at over four thousand years.

The greatness of what God has for His people is so great that the training program is extremely intense. The overall

---

267 Genesis 15:12-14
268 Exodus 16:35; Deuteronomy 8:2

Appendix E: Kings in Training

concept is that the greater the reward, the greater the discipline and training that is required. To teach someone to dig a ditch may take fifteen minutes, while training to be a doctor my take six years and longer. To become a joint-heir with Jesus Christ and a true son of God requires thousands of years of development, and for you and me, a life-time of detaching ourselves from the things of this world and attaching our mind, body, and spirit to the things of God.

Resources

BOOKS

REVELATION and the Age of The Antichrist – The book of Revelation is the timeline of earth's last seven years. Following the ordering of the book of Revelation, we also understand the ordering of last day events.

ARE WE THERE YET? – How close are we to the age of the Antichrist? Are We There Yet? Outlining the timelines recorded in Daniel, Matthew 24, and the book of Revelation, we can know where we are on the prophetic timeline and how close we are to the appearing of the Antichrist and the return of Christ.

COMING SOON – Understanding the last days does not have to be complicated. Jesus taught about the events characterizing the last days in 28 verses. This little book follows the ordering of events taught by Jesus to reveal the timeline to the arrival of the Antichrist, the return of Christ, and the rapture.

100% GUARANTEED: You Have An Appointment With Destiny – This forty-eight page book explores the evidence for God and eternity. It is an excellent follow up after sharing the Gospel, and a practical handbook that puts the essential arguments for God at a person's fingertip.

CHARTS

Chart of the Book of Revelation is companion to the book, "Revelation and the Age of the Antichrist." It outlines and follows the natural order of the revelation.

Chart of the Prophetic Timeline is companion to the books, "*Are We There Yet?*" and *"The Prophetic Timeline."*

STUDY GUIDES
100% Guaranteed: You Have An Appointment With Destiny

Resources may be downloaded at
www.ageofantichrist.com.

Contact, Speaking, &
Ordering Information

Age*of*Antichrist.*com*

ageofantichrist@outlook.com

AMAZON.com

Published by
Age*of*Antichirst.com
November 2017

Made in the USA
Columbia, SC
23 December 2022